W9-BAJ-161

Afghan Inspirations™

Publisher: Donna Robertson
Design Director: Fran Rohus
Production Director: Ange Van Arman

Editorial
Senior Editor: Jennifer Christiansen McClain
Editor: Sharon Lothrop
Associate Editors: Trudy Atteberry, Lyne Pickens, Jana Robertson

Photography
Photographers: Russell Chaffin, Keith Godfrey
Photography Coordinator/Stylist: Ruth Whitaker
Assistant Photo Stylist: Jan Jaynes
Cover Photograph: Keith Godfrey

Book Design/Production
Production Manager: Debby Keel
Color Specialist: Betty Radla

Product Design
Design Coordinator: Pam Prather

Business
CEO: John Robinson
Vice President/Marketing: Greg Deily • **Vice President/M.I.S.:** John Trotter

Credits
Sincerest thanks to all the designers, manufacturers and other professionals whose dedication has made this book possible.

Library of Congress Cataloging-in-Publication Data
ISBN: 1-57367-096-0
First Printing: 1997
Library of Congress Catalog Card Number: 97-68262
Published and Distributed by
The Needlecraft Shop, LLC, Big Sandy, Texas 75755
Printed in the United States of America.

Cover: *Secret Garden*, pattern begins on page 125.

Dear Friend,

The great writers of the past used ink and paper to immortalize the times of their lives, leaving a legacy that has endured for countless generations in the form of poetry and prose. Penned with hook and yarn instead, crochet offers that same lasting heritage — masterpieces reflecting an ages old art created to celebrate life in all its wonder. In this inspiring volume, you will find an exhilarating collection of designs worthy of a special, honored place in your heart and in your home.

With introductions taken from well-known authors setting the mood, each chapter is filled with a thought provoking selection of works by master crochet artisans. Exhibited in an unforgettable gallery format, these splendid examples of handiwork offer a unique array of choices for all your stitching desires.

Welcome to the grand gallery of crochet, and we hope you enjoy your visit.

Happy stitching,

Jennifer

Table of Contents

English Cottages

A Summer's Day

Rainbow in the Sky

Beautiful Things

Little One's Path

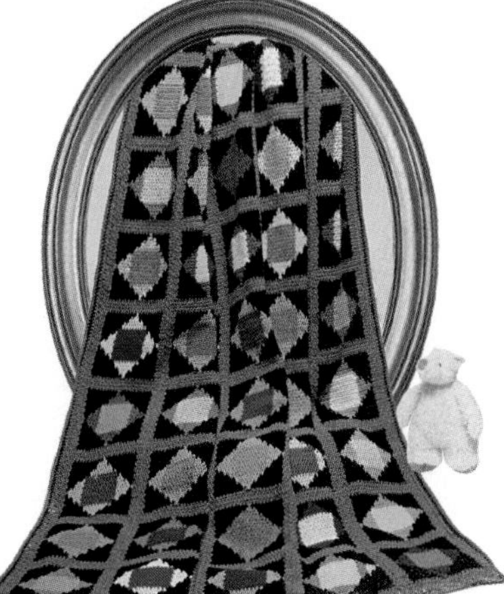

Celestial Light

Heaven in a Wildflower

My Garden

English Cottages

"…I travelled among unknown men
In lands beyond the sea;
Nor, England! did I know till then
What Love I bore to thee…"

—William Wordsworth

Heather Mist

Designer: Eleanor Albano-Miles

Size: 47" x 67".

Materials: Fuzzy sport yarn — 25 oz. ecru and 23 oz. pastel ombre; tapestry needle; I crochet hook or size needed to obtain gauge.

Gauge: 7 sc = 2"; 3 cluster rows and 2 sc rows = 2".

Skill Level: ★★ Average

INSTRUCTIONS

STRIP NO. 1 (make 3)

Row 1: With ombre, ch 16, sc in 2nd ch from hook, sc in each ch across, turn (15 sc).

NOTE: For **cluster (cl)**, yo, insert hook in next st, yo, draw lp through, yo, draw through 2 lps on hook, (yo, insert hook in same st, yo, draw lp through, yo, draw through 2 lps on hook) 2 times, yo, draw through all 4 lps on hook.

Row 2: Ch 1, sc in first st, (cl in next st, sc in next st) across, turn (8 sc, 7 cls).

Row 3: Ch 1, sc in each st across, turn.

Rows 4-15: Repeat rows 2 and 3 alternately At end of last row, fasten off.

Row 16: Join ecru with sc in first st, sc in each st across, turn.

Rows 17-20: Ch 1, sc in each st across, turn. At end of last row, fasten off.

Row 21: Join ombre with sc in first st, sc in each st across, turn.

NOTE: For **loop st (lp st),** insert hook in next st, wrap yarn 2 times around finger (see illustration), insert hook from left to right through all lps on finger, pull lps through st, drop lps from finger, yo, pull through all lps on hook.

LOOP STITCH

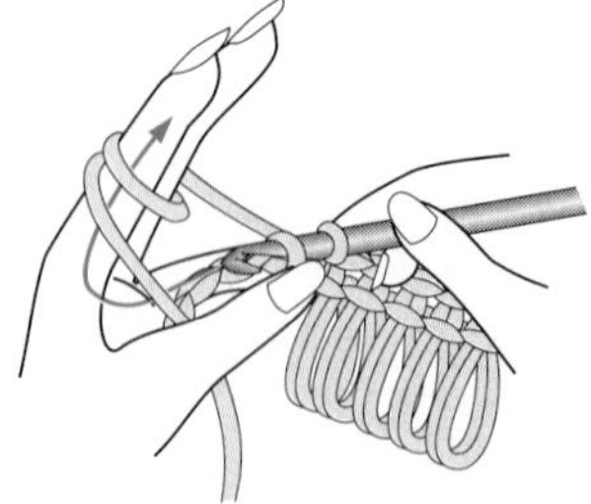

Row 22: Ch 1, sc in first st, lp st in each st across to last st, sc in last st, turn.

Rows 23-31: Repeat rows 3 and 22 alternately, ending with row 3. At end of last row, fasten off.

Rows 32-37: Repeat rows 16-21.

Rows 38-195: Repeat rows 2-37 consecutively, ending with row 15. At end of last row, **do not** turn.

Rnd 196: Working in rnds, join ecru with sc in first st, ch 2, sc in same st, sc in each st and in end of each row around with (sc, ch 2, sc) in each corner st, join with sl st in first sc, **turn** (17 sc on each short end between corner ch sps, 197 sc on each long edge between corner ch sps).

Rnd 197: Ch 4, (sc in next st, tr in next st) across to next corner ch sp, (sc, ch 2, sc) in next corner ch sp, *tr in next st, (sc in next st, tr in next st) across to next corner ch sp, (sc, ch 2, sc) in next corner ch sp; repeat from * 2 more times, join with sl st in top of ch-4, **turn.**

Rnd 198: Ch 1, sc in each st around with 3 sc in each corner ch sp, join with sl st in first sc, **turn,** fasten off.

Rnd 199: Join ombre with sl st in any st, ch 3, dc in each st around with (dc, ch 2, dc) in each center corner st, join with sl st in top of ch-3, **turn,** fasten off.

Rnd 200: Join ecru with sc in any corner ch sp, ch 2, sc in same sp, sc in each st around with (sc, ch 2, sc) in each corner ch sp, join, turn.

Rnds 201-202: Repeat rnds 197 and 198. At end of last rnd, **do not** turn or fasten off.

Rnd 203: Repeat rnd 198.

STRIP NO. 2 (make 2)

Row 1: With ecru, ch 16, sc in 2nd ch from hook, sc in each ch across, turn (15 sc).

Rows 2-5: Ch 1, sc in each st across, turn. At end of last row, fasten off.

Row 6: Join ombre with sc in first st, sc in each st across, turn.

Row 7: Ch 1, sc in first st, lp st in each st across to last st, sc in last st, turn.

Row 8: Ch 1, sc in each st across, turn.

Rows 9-16: Repeat rows 7 and 8 alternately. At end of last row, fasten off.

Continued on page 24

Lacy Trellis

Designer: Dot Drake

Size: 43" x 58½"
not including Fringe.

Materials: Worsted-weight yarn — 16 oz. each pink and green; G crochet hook or size needed to obtain gauge.

Gauge: 4 dc = 1"; 2 dc rows = 1¼".

Skill Level: ★★ Average

INSTRUCTIONS

FIRST STRIP

NOTES: For **shell,** (2 dc, ch 2, 2 dc) in next ch or ch sp.

For **picot,** ch 3, sl st in top of last st made.

Row 1: With green, ch 23, dc in 6th ch from hook, skip next 2 chs, shell in next ch, skip next 2 chs, dc in each of next 3 chs, picot, dc in each of next 3 chs, skip next 2 chs, shell in next ch, skip next 2 chs, dc in last ch, turn (8 dc, 2 shells).

Row 2: Ch 5, dc in first dc, shell in ch sp of next shell, ch 8, shell in ch sp of next shell, dc in last dc, turn. Ch 5, is not used or counted as a st.

Row 3: Ch 5, dc in first dc, shell in next shell, ch 6, shell in next shell, dc in last dc, turn.

Row 4: Ch 5, dc in first dc, shell in next shell, ch 3, sc around next chs of last 2 rows at same time, ch 3, shell in next shell, dc in last dc, turn.

Row 5: Ch 5, dc in first dc, shell in next shell, ch 3, tr in next sc, ch 3, shell in next shell, dc in last dc, turn.

Row 6: Ch 5, dc in first dc, shell in next shell, dc in each of next 3 chs, dc in next tr, picot, dc in each of next 3 chs, shell in next shell, dc in last dc, turn.

Rows 7-90: Repeat rows 2-6 consecutively, ending with row 5.

Row 91: Ch 5, dc in first dc, shell in next shell, dc in each of next 3 chs, dc in next tr, dc in each of next 3 chs, shell in next shell, dc in last dc, fasten off.

SECOND STRIP

Rows 1-91 With pink, repeat same rows of First Strip. At end of last row, **do not** turn or fasten off.

Row 92: To **join Strips,** ch 2, sc in first ch-5 sp on long edge of last Strip, (ch 2, sc in next ch-5 sp on this Strip, ch 2, sc in next ch-5 sp on last Strip) across, dc in first ch on opposite side of row 1 on this Strip, fasten off.

Alternating green and pink, repeat Second Strip six more times for a total of eight Strips.

FRINGE

For each **Fringe,** cut two strands each 12" long. With both strands held together, fold in half, insert hook in stitch, draw fold through stitch, draw all loose ends through fold, tighten. Trim ends.

Matching color of Strips, evenly space 11 Fringe across each end of each Strip.✣

A Baby Blessing

Tender Moments

Designer: Rosetta Harshman

Size: 38" x 48".

Materials: Fuzzy chunky yarn — 15 oz. each off-white and variegated; eight 9" lengths of 1/4" ribbon; tapestry needle; H crochet hook or size needed to obtain gauge.

Gauge: 7 sts = 2"; 2 dc rows = 1 1/4". Each Block is 5" square.

Skill Level: ★★ Average

INSTRUCTIONS

BLOCK NO. 1 (make 20)

Rnd 1: With off-white, ch 5, sl st in first ch to form ring, ch 3, 2 dc in ring, ch 2, (3 dc in ring, ch 2) 3 times, join with sl st in top of first ch-3 (12 dc, 4 ch-2 sps).

Rnd 2: Sl st in each of next 2 sts, sl st in next ch sp, (ch 3, 2 dc, ch 2, 3 dc) in same sp, ch 1, skip next st, dc in next st, *(3 dc, ch 2, 3 dc) in next ch sp, ch 1, skip next st, dc in next st; repeat from * around, join (28 dc, 4 ch sps).

Rnd 3: Ch 4, skip next st, *[dc in next st, *(2 dc, ch 2, 2 dc) in next ch sp, dc in next st, ch 1, skip next st, dc in next st], (ch 1, dc in next dc) 2 times, ch 1, skip next st; repeat from * 2 more times; repeat between [ ], ch 1, dc in next st, ch 1, join with sl st in 3rd ch of ch-4.

Rnd 4: Ch 4, dc in next st, *[ch 1, skip next st, dc in next st, (2 dc, ch 2, 2 dc) in next ch sp, dc in next dc, ch 1, skip next st, dc in next st], (ch 1, dc in next dc) 4 times; repeat from * 2 more times; repeat between [ ], (ch 1, dc in next st) 2 times, ch 1, join as before, fasten off.

BLOCK NO. 2 (make 43)

Rnds 1-3: With variegated, repeat same rnds as Block No. 1. At end of last rnd, fasten off.

Rnd 4: Join off-white with sl st in first st; repeat rnd 4 of Block No. 1.

Holding Blocks wrong sides together, matching sts; with off-white, sew together through **back lps** only according to Assembly Diagram.

EDGING

Rnd 1: Working around outer edge, join off-white with hdc in any corner ch sp, 4 hdc in same sp, hdc in each dc, hdc in each ch-1 sp, dc in each ch sp on each side of seams and 2 dc in each seam around with 5 hdc in each corner ch sp, join with sl st in top of first hdc, fasten off (143 sts on each short end between corner 5-hdc groups, 185 sts on each long edge between corner 5-hdc groups).

Rnd 2: Join variegated with sl st in center st of any corner 5-hdc group, ch 2, hdc in same st, hdc in each st around with 3 hdc in center st of each corner 5-hdc group, hdc in same st as first ch 2, join with sl st in top first ch-2 (149 hdc on each short end between center corner sts, 191 hdc on each long edge between center corner sts, 4 center corner sts).

Rnd 3: Ch 3, 5 dc in same st, *[skip next 2 sts, sc in next st, skip next 2 sts, (6 dc in next st, skip next 2 sts, sc in next st, skip next 2 sts) across] to next center corner st, 6 dc in next corner st; repeat from * 2 more times; repeat between [ ], join with sl st in top of ch-3, fasten off.

Tie pieces of ribbon to Afghan in bows as indicated on Assembly Diagram.✣

ASSEMBLY DIAGRAM

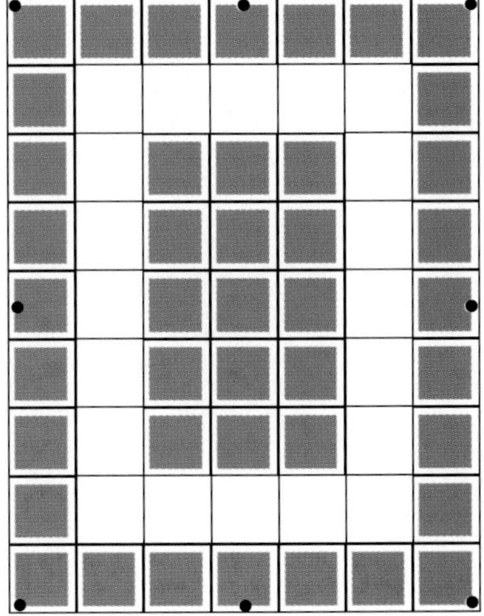

• = bow placement

Spring Compote

Designer: Jennifer Christiansen McClain

Size: 43" x 60", not including Fringe.

Materials: Worsted-weight yarn — 18 oz. pastel variegated, 15 oz. rose, 6 oz. each lilac and yellow; I and J crochet hooks or sizes needed to obtain gauges.

Gauges: **J hook,** 1 popcorn = 1" tall. **I hook,** 3 sts = 1".

Skill Level: ★★ Average

INSTRUCTIONS

STRIP (make 7)

NOTE: Leave 7" end when beginning and ending rows.

Center

Row 1: With J hook and rose; for **popcorn (pc),** *ch 4, 4 dc in 4th ch from hook, drop lp from hook, insert hook in top of ch-4, pull dropped lp through; repeat from * 51 more times, **do not** fasten off (52 pcs).

First Side Edging

NOTE: Work remainder of pattern with I hook.

Row 1: Ch 2, sc in 2nd ch from hook; working along side of Center, (ch 2, sc in next ch at bottom of pc) across, **do not** turn, fasten off (53 sc, 52 ch-2 sps).

Row 2: Join variegated with sl st in first sc, (3 dc in next ch-2 sp, sl st in next sc) across, fasten off (156 dc, 53 sl sts).

Row 3: Join lilac with sl st in first sl st, ch 3, 3 sc in center st of next 3-dc group, (ch 1, 3 sc in center st of next 3-dc group) across, dc in last sl st, fasten off (156 sc, 2 dc) First ch-3 counts as first dc.

Row 4: Join rose with sc in first dc, ch 1, skip next 2 sc, sc in next sc, (ch 1, skip next ch, sc in next sc, ch 1, skip next sc, sc in next sc) across to last 3-sc group, ch 1, skip next ch, sc in next sc, ch 1, skip next 2 sc, sc in last dc, fasten off (104 sc, 103 ch sps).

Row 5: Join yellow with sl st in first sc, (3 sc in next ch sp, ch 1, skip next ch sp) across to last ch sp, 3 sc in last ch sp, sl st in last sc, fasten off.

Row 6: Join variegated with sl st in first sl st, ch 3, skip next st, sc in next st; *working over ch-1 on last row, (dc, ch 1, dc) in skipped ch sp on row before last, skip next sc, sc in next sc; repeat from * across, dc in last sl st, fasten off.

Second Side Edging

Row 1: Working on opposite side of Center, join rose with sc in same ch as last sc on row 1 of First Side Edging, (ch 2, sc in same ch as next sc on First Edging) across, fasten off.

Rows 2-6: Repeat same rows of First Side Edging.

ASSEMBLY

Holding two Strips wrong sides together with center of Strips going in opposite directions, join rose with sc in first st of row 6 on Strip facing you, ch 1, sc in first st on other Strip, (ch 1, sc in next ch-1 sp on first Strip, ch 1, sc in next ch-1 sp on other Strip) across, ch 1, sc in last st on first Strip, ch 1, sc in last st on other Strip, fasten off.

Repeat until all Strips are joined.

OUTER EDGING

Working on one long outer edge, join rose with sc in first st, (ch 3, sc in next ch-1 sp) across, ch 3, sc in last st, fasten off.

Repeat on opposite edge.

FRINGE

For **each Fringe,** cut one 14" strand each color. With all strands held together, fold in half, insert hook in end of row, draw fold through, draw all loose ends and strands at end of row through fold, tighten. Trim ends.

Evenly space Fringe across each short end of Afghan.✣

Afternoon Tea

Designer: Jennifer Christiansen McClain

Size: 43" x 60".

Materials: Worsted-weight yarn — 16 oz. white, 14 oz. each pink and orchid; H crochet hook or size needed to obtain gauge.

Gauge: Rnds 1-3 = 3" across.

Skill Level: ★★ Average

INSTRUCTIONS

MOTIF A (make 24)

Rnd 1: With pink, ch 4, 15 dc in 4th ch from hook, join with sl st in top of ch-3 (16 dc).

Rnd 2: Ch 1, sc in first st, ch 3, skip next st, (sc in next st, ch 3, skip next st) around, join with sl st in first sc, fasten off (8 ch sps, 8 sc).

Rnd 3: Join white with sc in any sc; working behind ch-3 sps of last rnd in skipped sts of rnd before last, 3 dc in next skipped st, (sc in next sc on last rnd, 3 dc in next skipped st on rnd before last) around, join (24 dc, 8 sc).

Rnd 4: Ch 1, sc in first st, ch 3, skip next st, (sc in next st, ch 3, skip next st) around, join, fasten off (16 ch sps).

Rnd 5: Working behind ch-3 sps on last nrd in skipped sts on rnd before last, join orchid with sl st in any skipped st, ch 3, sc around adjacent ch-3 lp on last rnd, dc in same st as ch-3, (dc in next skipped st, sc around adjacent ch-3 lp, dc in same st as last dc) around, join with sl st in top of ch-3 (32 dc, 16 sc).

Rnd 6: Ch 1, sc in first st, ch 2, skip next sc, (sc in each of next 2 dc, ch 2, skip next sc) around to last dc, sc in last dc, join with sl st in first sc, fasten off (16 ch-2 sps).

Rnd 7: Join white with sl st in any ch-2 sp, ch 3, 2 dc in same ch sp; for **petals,** (sl st, ch 3, 2 dc) in each ch-2 sp around, join with sl st in first sl st, fasten off (16 petals).

Rnd 8: Join pink with sl st in **back lp** of any sl st, ch 3, (sl st in **back lp** of next sl st, ch 3) around, join with sl st in first sl st (16 ch-3 sps).

Rnd 9: Ch 1, sc in same sl st, *[(2 sc, hdc, dc) in next ch sp, (2 dc, 2 tr) in next ch sp, (tr, ch 2, tr) in next sl st, (2 tr, 2 dc) in next ch sp, (dc, hdc, 2 sc) in next ch sp], sc in next sl st; repeat from * 2 more times; repeat between [ ], join with sl st in first sc, fasten off (19 sts on each side between ch-2 sps).

Rnd 10: Join white with sc in any corner ch sp, (sc, ch 2, 2 sc) in same sp, sc in each st around with (2 sc, ch 2, 2 sc) in each ch sp, join, fatten off (23 sts each side).

MOTIF B (make 24)

Work same as Motif A, reversing pink and orchid.

ASSEMBLY

Holding one Motif A and one Motif B with right sides together, join white with sc in first corner ch sp, sc in each st across to next corner ch sp, sc in corner ch sp, ch 1; holding 2 more Motifs with right sides together, sc in first corner ch sp, sc in each st across to next ch sp, sc in next ch sp. Alternating Motifs, continue joining in same manner until 16 Motifs are joined in two strips of eight Motifs each, fasten off.

Repeat with remaining Motifs, making a total of six Strips of eight Motifs each. Working horizontally across strips, join remaining edges in same manner.

BORDER

Rnd 1: Working around outer edge, join white with sc in any corner ch sp, 2 sc in same sp, sc in each st around with hdc in each seam and 3 sc in each corner ch sp, join with sl st in first sc (680 sts).

Rnd 2: Ch 3, 2 dc in same st, skip next 2 sts, *(sl st, ch 3, 2 dc) in next st, skip next 2 sts; repeat from * around to last 2 sts, (sl st ch 3, 2 dc) in next st, skip last st, join with sl st in joining sl st of last rnd, fasten off.✣

England

Morning Glory

Designer: Carol Smith

Size: 51" x 74".

Materials: Worsted-weight yarn — 16 oz. each green and white, 8 oz. each lt. burgundy, dk. burgundy, lt. blue and dk. blue; I crochet hook or size needed to obtain gauge.

Gauge: Rnds 1-2 of Motif = 2½" across.

Skill Level: ★★★ Advanced

INSTRUCTIONS

FIRST ROW

First Motif

Rnd 1: With white, ch 4, sl st in first ch to form ring, ch 3, 11 dc in ring, join with sl st in top of ch-3, fasten off (12 dc).

NOTES: For **treble front post stitch (tr fp)** (see figure 9, page 159), yo 2 times, insert hook from right to left around post of st on previous row, complete as tr.

For **picot,** ch 3, sl st in top of last st made.

Rnd 2: Join lt. blue with sl st in any st, ch 3, dc in same st, tr fp around next st, (2 dc in next st, tr fp around next st) around, join, fasten off (18 sts).

Rnd 3: Join dk. blue with sl st in first st, dc in same st, 2 dc in next st, tr fp around next tr fp, picot, (2 dc in each of next 2 sts, tr fp around next tr fp, picot) around, join, fasten off (30 sts, 6 picots).

Rnd 4: Working this rnd in **back lps** only, join white with sc in first st; skipping picots, sc in next 4 sts, ch 1, (sc in next 5 sts, ch 1) around, join with sl st in first sc, fasten off. Pull picots to front of work.

Rnd 5: Working this rnd in **back lps** only, join green with sl st in any ch sp, ch 3, dc in next 5 sts, ch 3, (sl st in next ch-1 sp, ch 3, dc in next 5 sts, ch 3) around, join with sl st in first sl st.

Rnd 6: (*Ch 3, sl st in next dc, ch 3, dc in each of next 3 sts, ch 3, sl st in next st, ch 3*, sl st in next sl st) 5 times; repeat between **, join with sl st in joining sl st of last rnd.

Rnd 7: *[Ch 3, sl st in next sl st, ch 3, sl st in next dc, dc in next dc, ch 3, sl st in next dc], (ch 3, sl st in next sl st) 2 times; repeat from * 4 more times; repeat between [ ], ch 3, sl st in next sl st, ch 3, join as before, fasten off.

Rnd 8: Join white with sc in first ch-3 sp, ch 3, (sc in next ch-3 sp, ch 3) around, join with sl st in first sc, fasten off (36 ch sps).

Second Motif

Rnds 1-7: Substituting lt. and dk. burgundy for lt. and dk. blue, repeat same rnds of First Motif.

Rnd 8: Join white with sc in first ch-3 sp, (ch 3, sc in next ch-3 sp) 2 times; to **join,** *ch 1, sl st in corresponding ch-3 sp on last Motif (see Assembly Diagram on page 25), ch 1, sc in next ch-3 sp on this Motif, ch 1, sl st in next ch-3 sp on other Motif, ch 1, sc in next ch-3 sp on this Motif*, (ch 3, sc in next ch-3 sp) 3 times; repeat between **, ch 3, (sc in next ch-3 sp, ch 3) around, join with sl st in first sc, fasten off.

Alternating colors of Motifs according to Assembly Diagram, repeat Second Motif three more times for a total of five Motifs. (Half Motifs are added last.)

SECOND ROW

First Motif

Rnds 1-7: Substituting lt. and dk. burgundy for lt. and dk. blue, repeat same rnds of First Motif.

Rnd 8: Join white with sc in first ch-3 sp, (ch 3, sc in next ch-3 sp) 2 times; to **join,** *ch 1, sl st in corresponding ch-3 sp of First Motif on row above (see Joining Diagram), ch 1, sc in next ch-3 sp on this Motif, ch 1, sl st in next ch-3 sp on other Motif, ch 1, sc in next ch-3 sp on this Motif*, (ch 3, sc in next ch-3 sp) 3 times, ch 1, sl st in corresponding ch-3 sp on other Motif, ch 1, sc in next ch-3 sp on this Motif, ch 1, sl st around joining sl st between joined Motifs on row above, ch 1, sc in next ch-3 sp on this Motif, ch 1, sl st in corresponding ch sp of next Motif on row above, ch 1, sc in next ch sp on this Motif, (ch 3, sc in next ch sp) 3 times; working on same Motif as last joining, repeat between **, ch 3, (sc in

Continued on page 20

Morning Glory

continued from page 19

next ch sp, ch 3) around, join with sl st in first sc, fasten off.

Second Motif

Rnds 1-7: Repeat same rnds of First Motif.

Rnd 8: Join white with sc in first ch-3 sp, (ch 3, sc in next ch-3 sp) 2 times; to **join,** *ch 1, sl st in corresponding ch-3 sp of last Motif on this row, ch 1, sc in next ch-3 sp on this Motif, ch 1, sl st in next ch-3 sp on other Motif, ch 1, sc in next ch-3 sp on this Motif*, (ch 3, sc in next ch-3 sp) 3 times, ch 1, sl st in corresponding ch-3 sp on other Motif, ch 1, sc in next ch-3 sp on this Motif, ch 1, sl st around joining sl st between last Motif on this row and next Motif on row above, ch 1, sc in next ch-3 sp on this Motif, ch 1, sl st in corresponding ch sp of Motif on row above, ch 1, sc in next ch sp on this Motif, (ch 3, sc in next ch sp) 3 times, ch 1, sl st in corresponding ch-3 sp on other Motif, ch 1, sc in next ch-3 sp on this Motif, ch 1, sl st around joining sl st between joined Motifs on row above, ch 1, sc in next ch-3 sp on this Motif, ch 1, sl st in corresponding ch sp of next Motif on row above, ch 1, sc in next ch sp on this Motif, (ch 3, sc in next ch sp) 3 times, ch 1, sl st in corresponding ch sp of Motif on row above, ch 1, sc in next ch sp on this Motif, ch 1, sl st in in next ch sp of other Motif, ch 1, sc in next ch sp on this Motif, ch 3, (sc in next ch sp, ch 3) around, join with sl st in first sc, fasten off.

Third Motif

With burgundy, work same as Second Row Second Motif.

Fourth Motif

Work same as Second Row Second Motif.

Fifth Motif

Rnds 1-7: Substituting burgundy for blue, repeat same rnds of First Motif.

Rnd 8: Join white with sc in first ch-3 sp, (ch 3, sc in next ch-3 sp) 2 times; to **join,** *ch 1, sl st in corresponding ch-3 sp of last Motif on this row, ch 1, sc in next ch-3 sp on this Motif, ch 1, sl st in next ch-3 sp on other Motif, ch 1, sc in next ch-3 sp on this Motif*, (ch 3, sc in next ch-3 sp) 3 times, ch 1, sl st in corresponding ch-3 sp on other Motif, ch 1, sc in next ch-3 sp on this Motif, ch 1, sl st around joining sl st between last Motif on this row and next Motif on row above, ch 1, sc in next ch-3 sp on this Motif, ch 1, sl st in corresponding ch sp of Motif on row above, ch 1, sc in next ch sp on this Motif, (ch 3, sc in next ch sp) 3 times, ch 1, sl st in corresponding ch-3 sp on other Motif, ch 1, sc in next ch-3 sp on this Motif, ch 1, sl st around joining sl st between joined Motifs on row above, ch 1, sc in next ch-3 sp on this Motif, ch 1, sl st in corresponding ch sp of next Motif on row above, ch 1, sc in next ch sp on this Motif, ch 3, (sc in next ch sp, ch 3) around, join with sl st in first sc, fasten off.

THIRD ROW

First Motif

With lt. and dk. blues, joining to last Motif on row above, work same as First Row Second Motif.

Second–Fifth Motifs

Alternating colors as shown in Assembly Diagram, work same as Second Row Second Motif.

Alternating blue and burgundy Motifs, repeat Second Motif three more times for a total of five Motifs.

Repeat Second and Third rows alternately for a total of nine rows.

FOURTH–NINTH ROWS

Alternating colors as shown, repeat Second and Third Rows alternately.

FIRST HALF MOTIF

Row 1: With white, ch 4, sl st in first ch to form ring, ch 3, 6 dc in ring, **do not** turn, fasten off (7 dc).

Row 2: Join lt. burgundy with sl st in first st, ch 3, dc in same st, tr fp around next st, (2 dc in next st, tr fp around next st) 2 times, 2 dc last st, fasten off (11 sts).

Row 3: Join dk. burgundy with sl st in first st, ch 3, dc in next st, tr fp around next tr fp, picot, (2 dc in each of next 2 sts, tr fp around next tr fp, picot) 2 times, dc in each of last 2 sts, fasten off (15 sts, 3 picots).

Row 4: Working this row in **back lps** only, join white with sc in first st, sc in next st, ch 1, skip next tr fp, (sc in next 5 sts, ch 1) 2 times, sc in each of last 2 sts, fasten off (14 sc, 3 ch-1 sps).

Row 5: Working this row in **back lps** only, join green with sl st in first st, ch 3, dc in next st, ch 3, sl st in next ch-1 sp, (ch 3, dc in next 5 sts, ch 3, sl st in next ch-1 sp) 2 times, ch 3, dc in each of last 2 sts, turn.

Row 6: Ch 3, dc in next st, ch 3, sl st in first ch of next ch-3, (ch 3, sl st in next sl st, ch 3, sl st in next dc, ch 3, dc in each of next 3 sts, ch 3, sl st in next dc) 2 times, ch 3, sl st in next sl st, ch 3, sl st in 3rd ch of next ch-3, ch 3, dc in each of last 2 sts, turn.

Row 7: Ch 6, sl st in next dc, *(ch 3, sl st in next sl st) 3 times, ch 3, sl st in next dc, ch 3, dc in next dc, ch 3, sl st in next dc; repeat from *, (ch 3, sl st in next sl st) 3 times, ch 3, sl st in next dc, ch 3, dc in last st, **do not** turn, fasten off.

Rnd 8: Working around entire outer edge in sts and in ends of rows, join white with sc in ring on opposite side of row 1, ch 3, skip first row, sc in next row, ch 3, sc in next row, ch 3, skip next row, sc in next row, ch 3, sc in next row, ch 3, (sc, ch 3, sc) in next ch sp, (ch 3, sc in next ch sp) 5 times, ch 1, sl st in corresponding ch sp on Motif (see Assembly Diagram), ch 1, sc in next ch sp on this Motif, ch 1, sl st in next ch sp on other Motif, ch 1, sc in next ch sp on this Motif, (ch 3, sc in next ch sp) 3 times, ch 1, sl st in corresponding ch-3 sp on other Motif, ch 1, sc in next ch-3 sp on this Motif, ch 1, sl st around joining sl st between joined Motifs on row above, ch 1, sc in next ch-3 sp on this Motif, ch 1, sl st in corresponding ch sp of next Motif on row above, ch 1, sc in next ch sp on this Motif, (ch 3, sc in next ch sp) 3 times, ch 1, sl st in corresponding ch sp on other Motif, ch 1, sc in next ch sp on this Motif, ch 1, sl st in corresponding ch sp on other Motif, ch 1, sc in **same** ch sp on this Motif, (ch 3, sc in next row) 2 times, ch 3, skip next row, sc in next row, ch 3, sc in next row, ch 3, skip last row, join with sl st in first sc, fasten off.

SECOND HALF MOTIF

Rows 1-7: Repeat same rows of First Half Motif.

Rnd 8: Working around entire outer edge in sts and in ends of rows, join white with sc in ring on opposite side of row 1, ch 3, skip first row, sc in next row, ch 3, sc in next row, ch 3, skip next row, sc in next row, ch 3, sc in next row, ch 3, sc in next ch sp, ch 1, sl st in corresponding ch sp on Motif (see Assembly Diagram), ch 1, sc in same ch sp on this Motif, ch 1, sl st in next ch sp on other Motif, ch 1, sc in next ch sp on this Motif, (ch 3, sc in next ch sp) 3 times, *ch 1, sl st in corresponding ch-3 sp on other Motif, ch 1, sc in next ch-3 sp on this Motif, ch 1, sl st around joining sl st between Motifs, ch 1, sc in next ch-3 sp on this Motif, ch 1, sl st in corresponding ch sp of next Motif, ch 1, sc in next ch sp on this Motif, (ch 3, sc in next ch sp) 3 times; repeat from *, (ch 3, sc in next ch sp) 3 times, ch 1, sl st in corresponding ch sp on other Motif, ch 1, sc in next ch sp on this Motif, ch 1, sl st in next ch sp on other Motif, ch 1, sc in same ch sp on this Motif, (ch 3, sc in next row) 2 times, ch 3, skip next row, sc in next row, ch 3, sc in next row, ch 3, skip last row, join with sl st in first sc, fasten off.

Repeat Second Half Motif two more times according to Assembly Diagram.

LAST BURGUNDY HALF MOTIF

Rows 1-7: Repeat same rows of First Half Motif.

Rnd 8: Working around entire outer edge in sts and in ends of rows, join white with sc in ring on opposite side of row 1, ch 3, skip first row, sc in next row, ch 3, sc in next row, ch 3, skip next row, sc in next row, ch 3, sc in next row, ch 3, sc in next ch sp, ch 1, sl st in corresponding ch sp on Motif (see Assembly Diagram), ch 1, sc in same ch sp on this Motif, ch 1, sl st in next ch sp on other Motif, ch 1, sc in next ch sp on this Motif, (ch 3, sc in next ch sp) 3 times, *ch 1, sl st in corresponding ch-3 sp on other Motif, ch 1, sc in next ch-3 sp on this Motif, ch 1, sl st around joining sl st between Motifs, ch 1, sc in next ch-3 sp on this Motif, ch 1, sl st in corresponding ch sp of next Motif, ch 1, sc in next ch sp on this Motif, (ch 3, sc in next ch sp) 3 times, ch 1, sl st in corresponding ch sp on other Motif, ch 1, sc in next ch sp on this Motif, ch 1, sl st in next ch sp on other Motif, ch 1, sc in next ch sp on this Motif, (ch 3, sc in next ch sp) 4 times, ch 3, (sc, ch 3, sc) in next ch sp, (ch 3, sc in next row) 2 times, ch 3, skip next row, sc in next row, ch 3, sc in next row, ch 3, skip last row, join with sl st in first sc, fasten off.

BLUE HALF MOTIFS

Working on opposite side of afghan as shown in Assembly Diagram, work same as Second Half Motif.

BORDER

Rnd 1: Join white with sc in ch sp of top right corner point as indicated on Assembly Diagram, ch 3, sc in same sp, *ch 3, (sc in next ch sp, ch 3) 5 times, (sc, ch 3, sc) in next ch sp, ch 3, (sc in next ch sp, ch 3) 5 times, sc around joining sl st*; repeat between ** 4 more times, ch 3, (sc in next ch sp, ch 3) 5 times, (sc, ch 3, sc) in next ch sp, ◊ch 3, (sc in next ch sp, ch 3) 10 times, sc around next joining sl st, ch 3, (sc in next ch sp, ch 3) 5 times, sc around next joining sl st◊; repeat between ◊◊ 3 more times, ch 3, (sc in next ch sp, ch 3) 10 times, [(sc, ch 3, sc) in next ch sp, ch 3, (sc in next ch sp, ch 3) 5 times, sc around joining sl st, ch 3, (sc in next ch sp, ch 3) 5 times]; repeat between [ ] 4 more times, (sc, ch 3, sc) in next ch sp, ch 3, (sc in next ch sp, ch 3) 5 times, (sc, ch 3, sc) in next ch sp, ch 3, (sc in next ch sp, ch 3) 5 times, sc around joining sl st; repeat between ◊◊ 4 more times, join with sl st in first sc.

Rnd 2: (Sl st, ch 1, sc, ch 3, sc) in first ch sp, ch 3, (sc, ch 3) in each ch sp around with (sc, ch 3, sc, ch 3) in each ch sp at points, join.

NOTE: For **shell,** (3 dc, ch 1, 3 dc) in next ch sp.

Rnd 3: This rnd is worked in four Sections, A, B, C and D; when working each section, repeat

Continued on page 25

Dresden Plate

Designer: Brenda Stratton

for Monsanto's Designs for America Program

Size: 53" x 70".

Materials: Worsted-weight yarn — 34 oz. white, 1¼ oz. each lt. turquoise, dk. turquoise, lt. berry, dk. berry, lt. jade, dk. jade, lt. country blue, dk. county blue, brown, tan, purple, lavender, lt. olive, dk. olive, lt. terracotta, dk. terracotta, lt royal blue, dk. royal blue, dk. rose and lt rose; tapestry needle; G crochet hook or size needed to obtain gauge.

Guage: 4 sc sts = 1", 4 sc rows = 1". Block center = 2¼" across.

Skill Level: ★★ Average

INSTRUCTIONS

BLOCK (make 12)

Wedge (make 12, see Note)

NOTE: For each Block, make 12 Wedges, 6 each of light and dark colors in the following color combinations: lt. turquoise/dk. turquoise, lt. berry/dk. berry, lt. jade/dk. jade, lt. plum/dk. plum, lt. teal/ dk. teal, lt. country blue/dk. country blue, tan/brown, lavender/purple, lt. olive/dk. olive, lt. terracotta/dk. terracotta, lt. royal blue/dk. royal blue, lt. rose/dk. rose.

Row 1: Ch 4, sc in 2nd ch from hook, sc in each ch across, turn (3 sc).

Row 2: Ch 1, sc in first st; for **increase,** 2 sc in next st; sc in last st, turn (4 sc).

Row 3: Ch 1, sc in each st across with 2 sc in 2nd st of 2-sc increase, turn (5).

Row 4: Ch 1, sc in each st across, turn.

Rows 5-21: Repeat rows 3 and 4 alternately, ending with row 3 and 14 sts.

Row 22: Sl st in first st, hdc in each of next 3 sts, dc in each of next 2 sts, 2 dc in each of next 2 sts, dc in each of next 2 sts, hdc in each of next 3 sts, sl st in last st, fasten off (16 sts).

To **join,** alternating lt. and dk. colors, with right sides held together, sl st Wedges together across ends of rows.

Center

NOTE: Do not join rnds unless otherwise stated. Mark first st of each rnd.

Rnd 1: With white, ch 2, 6 sc in 2nd ch from hook (6 sc).

Rnd 2: 2 sc in each st around (12).

Rnd 3: (Sc in next st, 2 sc in next st) around (18).

Rnd 4: (Sc in each of next 2 sts, 2 sc in next st) around, join with sl st in first sc, **do not** fasten off (24).

To **join,** sl st Center to inside opening on Wedges working in 2 sts of each Wedge.

Edging

Rnd 1: Working around outer edge, join white with sc in first st of row 22 on any Wedge, [*ch 1, skip next st, sc in next st, ch 2, skip next st, (sc in next st, ch 1, skip next st, sc in next st, ch 2, skip next st) 3 times], sc in next st on next Wedge; repeat from * 10 more times; repeat between [ ], join with sl st in first sc (96 ch sps).

Rnd 2: Sl st in first ch sp, ch 1, sc in same sp, (ch 2, sc in next ch sp) 3 times, [*ch 3, sc in next ch sp, (ch 3, skip next ch sp, sc in next ch sp) 3 times, (ch 3, sc in next ch sp) 3 times, (ch 3, skip next ch sp, sc in next ch sp) 3 times, ch 3, sc in next ch sp], (ch 2, sc in next ch sp) 7 times; repeat from * 2 more times; repeat between [ ], ch 2, (sc in next ch sp, ch 2) 3 times, join (72 ch sps).

Rnd 3: Sl st in first ch sp, ch 1, 2 sc in same sp, sc in next ch sp, 2 sc in each of next 2 ch sps, [*4 dc in next ch sp, 3 tr in each of next 3 ch sps, 5 tr in next ch sp, 3 tr in each of next 3 ch sps, 4 dc in next ch sp], (sc in next ch sp, 2 sc in each of next 2 ch sps) 3 times; repeat from * 2 more times; repeat between [ ], sc in next ch sp, 2 sc in each of next 2 ch sps, sc in next ch sp, 2 sc in last ch sp, join (184 sts).

NOTE: For **double treble crochet (dtr),** yo 3 times, insert hook in next st, yo, draw lp through, (yo, draw through 2 lps on hook) 4 times.

Rnd 4: Ch 1, sc in first 10 sts, [*hdc in next st,

Continued on page 24

Dresden Plate

continued from page 23

dc in each of next 3 sts, tr in each of next 3 sts, dtr in next 5 sts, 5 dtr in next st, dtr in next 5 sts, tr in each of next 3 sts, dc in each of next 3 sts, hdc in next st], sc in next 21 sts; repeat from * 2 more times; repeat between [ ], sc in last 11 sts, join (200 sts).

Rnd 5: Ch 2, hdc in next 18 sts, [*dc in next 5 sts; for **corner,** 5 dc in next st; dc in next 5 sts], hdc in next 39 sts; repeat from * 2 more times; repeat between [ ], hdc in last 20 sts, join with sl st in top of ch-2 (216 sts).

Rnd 6: Ch 3, dc in each st around with (2 dc, ch 1, 2 dc) in center st of each 5-dc corner group, join with sl st in top of ch-3, fasten off (228 dc, 4 ch-1 sps).

Holding Blocks wrong sides together, matching sts, with white, sew together in three rows of four Blocks each arranging as desired.

BORDER

Rnd 1: Working around entire outer edge of Blocks, join white with sl st in corner ch-1 sp before one short end, ch 3, (dc, ch 1, 2 dc) in same sp, dc in each st and in each seam across to next corner ch-1 sp, *(2 dc, ch 1, 2 dc) in next corner ch-1 sp, dc in each st and in each seam across to next corner ch-1 sp; repeat from * around, join with sl st in top of ch-3 (177 dc across each short end, 235 dc across each long edge, 4 corner ch-1 sps).

Rnd 2: Ch 3, dc in each st around with (2 dc, ch 1, 2 dc) in each corner ch-1 sp, join (181 dc across each short end, 239 dc across each long edge, 4 corner ch 1 sps).

Rnd 3: Sl st in each of next 3 sts, sl st in next ch-1 sp, ch 3, 6 dc in same sp, *skip next 3 sts, sl st in next st, skip next 3 sts, (7 dc in next st, skip next 2 sts, sl st in next st, skip next 2 sts) across to next corner ch-1 sp, 7 dc in next corner ch-1 sp, skip next 2 sts, sl st in next st, skip next 2 sts; repeat between ( ) across to next corner ch-1 sp*, 7 dc in next corner ch-1 sp; repeat between **, join, fasten off.✥

Heather Mist

continued from page 8

Row 17: Join ecru with sc in first st, sc in each st across, turn.

Rows 18-22: Repeat rows 2-6.

Row 23: Ch 1, sc in first st, (cl in next st, sc in next st) across, turn (8 sc, 7 cls).

Row 24: Ch 1, sc in each st across, turn.

Rows 25-36: Repeat rows 23 and 24 alternately. At end of last row, fasten off.

Row 37: Join ecru with sc in first st, sc in each st across, turn.

Rows 38-201: Repeat rows 2-37 consecutively, ending with row 21. At end of last row, **do not** fasten off.

Rnd 202: Ch 1, sc in first st, ch 2, sc in same st, sc in each st and in end of each row around with (sc, ch 2, sc) in each corner st, join with sl st in first sc, **turn** (17 sc on each short end between corner ch sps, 203 sc on each long edge between corner ch sps).

Rnds 203-209: Repeat rnds 197-203 of Strip No. 1.

Beginning with Strip No. 1 and alternating direction of Strips No. 1 and No. 2, with ecru, easing to fit, sew long edges together through **back bars** (see illustration).

EDGING

Join ombre with sc in any st, working left to right, **reverse sc** (see figure 10, page 159) in each st and in each seam around, join, fasten off.✥

BACK BAR OF SC

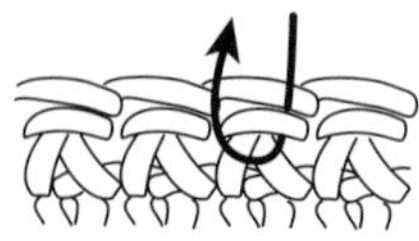

Morning Glory

continued from page 21

only instructions from that section unless otherwise stated.

Section A: Sl st in first ch sp, (ch 3, 2 dc, ch 1, 3 dc) in same sp, (3 dc in next ch sp, sc in next ch sp) 3 times, 3 dc in next ch sp, *shell in next ch sp, (3 dc in next ch sp, sc in next ch sp) 3 times, sc in each of next 2 ch sps, (3 dc in next ch sp, sc in next ch sp) 2 times, 3 dc in next ch sp; repeat from * 4 more times, shell in next ch sp;

Section B: (3 dc in next ch sp, sc in next ch sp) 2 times, 3 dc in next ch sp, *[shell in next ch sp, sc in next sc, shell in next ch sp, (3 dc in next ch sp, sc in next ch sp) 2 times], shell in next ch sp, (sc in next ch sp, 3 dc in next ch sp) 2 times, sc in next ch sp, shell in next ch sp, (sc in next ch sp, 3 dc in next ch sp) 2 times; repeat from * 3 more times; repeat between [ ], 3 dc in next ch sp, shell in next ch sp;

Section C: (3 dc in next ch sp, sc in next ch sp) 3 times, sc in each of next 2 ch sps, (3 dc in next ch sp, sc in next ch sp) 2 times, 3 dc in next ch sp, shell in next ch sp; repeat from * 4 more times, shell in next ch sp, (3 dc in next ch sp, sc in next ch sp) 3 times, 3 dc in next ch sp, shell in next ch sp;

Section D: (3 dc in next ch sp, sc in next ch sp) 3 times, shell in next ch sp, (sc in next ch sp, 3 dc in next ch sp) 2 times, *[shell in next ch sp, ch 1, sc in next sc, ch 1, shell in next ch sp, (3 dc in next ch sp, sc in next ch sp) 2 times, shell in next ch sp, (sc in next ch sp, 3 dc in next ch sp) 2 times, sc in next ch sp], shell in next ch sp, (sc in next ch sp, 3 dc in next ch sp) 2 times; repeat from * 2 more times; repeat between [ ], 3 dc in last ch sp, join with sl st in top of ch-3, fasten off.✣

ASSEMBLY DIAGRAM

Last Burgundy Half Motif

Begin Border Here

First Row First Motif

Second Row First Motif

Second Half Motif

First Half Motif

A Summer's Day

"Shall I compare thee to a summer's day?
Thou art more lovely and more temperate:
Rough winds do shake the darling buds of May,
And summer's lease hath all too short a date; . . ."

—William Shakespeare

Rippling Brook

Designer: *Anne Halliday*

for Monsanto's Designs for America Program

Size: 44" x 64" not including Fringe.

Materials: Worsted-weight yarn — 18 oz. white, 14 oz. each med. blue and lt. blue, 11 oz. each dk. blue and pale blue; G crochet hook or size needed to obtain gauge.

Gauge: 4 sts and 4 chs = 2"; 4 sc rows = 1".

Skill Level: ★ Easy

INSTRUCTIONS

AFGHAN

Row 1: With white, ch 172, sc in 2nd ch from hook, (ch 1, skip next ch, sc in next ch) across, turn, fasten off (86 sc, 85 ch sps).

Row 2: Join dk. blue with sc in first st, ch 1, 3 dc in next ch sp, ch 1, *(sc in next st, ch 1) 4 times, 3 dc in next ch sp, ch 1; repeat from * across to last st, sc in last st, turn, fasten off.

Row 3: Skipping ch-1 sps and 3-dc groups, join white with sc in first sc, (ch 1, sc in next sc) across, turn, fasten off.

Row 4: Skipping ch-1 sps, join med. blue with sc in first st, ch 1, dc in each of next 3 dc on row before last, ch 1, *(sc in next sc, ch 1) 4 times, 3 dc in each of next 3 dc on row before last, ch 1; repeat from* across to last sc, sc in last sc, turn, fasten off.

Rows 5-253: Working in color sequence of white, lt. blue, white, pale blue, white, lt. blue, white, med. blue, white and dk. blue, white, med. blue, repeat rows 3 and 4 alternately, ending with row 3.

Row 254: Join dk. blue with sc in first st, ch 1, dc next 3 dc on row before last tog, ch 1, *(sc in next sc, ch 1) 4 times, dc next 3 dc on row before last tog, ch 1; repeat from * across to last sc, sc in last sc, turn, fasten off.

Row 255: Skipping ch-1 sps and dc, join white with sc in first sc, (ch 1, sc in next sc) across, turn, fasten off.

Row 256: Join dk. blue with sl st in first st, (ch 1, skip next ch-1 sp, sl st in next st) across, fasten off.

Row 257: Working in starting ch on opposite side of row 1, join dk. blue with sl st in first ch, (ch 1, skip next ch, sl st in next ch) across, fasten off.

AFGHAN

For **each Fringe,** cut seven strands dk. blue each 12" long. With all strands held together, fold in half, insert hook through st below 3-dc group, draw fold through, draw all loose ends through fold, tighten, trim ends.

Fringe st below each 3-dc group on each short end of Afghan.✣

Creme de Menthe

Designer: Wilma Pelley

of Carol Alexander Design Studios for Monsanto's Designs for America Program

Size: 43" x 53" not including Fringe.

Materials: Worsted-weight yarn — 21 oz. each jade and snow white; H crochet hook or size needed to obtain gauge.

Gauge: 7 dc = 2"; 2 dc rows = 1".

Skill Level: ★★ Average

INSTRUCTIONS

JADE STRIP (make 4)

Row 1: With jade, ch 21, sc in 2nd ch from hook, sc in each ch across, turn (20 sc).

NOTE: When changing colors (see figure 11, page 159), always drop all colors to same side of work. Carry dropped color across to next section of same color.

Row 2: Ch 3 changing to white in last ch made, dc in each of next 2 sts changing to jade in last st made, dc in next 14 sts changing to white in last st made, dc in each of next 2 sts changing to jade in last st made, dc in last st, turn.

Row 3: Ch 3, dc in each of next 2 sts changing to white in last st made, dc in each of next 2 sts changing to jade in last st made, dc in next 10 sts changing to white in last st made, dc in each of next 2 sts changing to jade in last st made, dc in each of last 3 sts, turn.

Row 4: Ch 3, dc in next 4 sts changing to white in last st made, dc in each of next 2 sts changing to jade in last st made, dc in next 6 sts changing to white in last st made, dc in each of next 2 sts changing to jade in last st made, dc in last 5 sts, turn.

Row 5: Ch 3, dc in next 6 sts changing to white in last st made, dc in each of next 2 sts changing to jade in last st made, dc in each of next 2 sts changing to white in last st made, dc in each of next 2 sts changing to jade in last st made, dc in last 7 sts, turn.

Row 6: Ch 3, dc in next 8 sts changing to white in last st made, dc in each of next 2 sts changing to jade in last st made, dc in last 9 sts, turn.

Row 7: Repeat row 5.

Row 8: Repeat row 4.

Row 9: Repeat row 3.

Rows 10-106: Repeat rows 2-9 consecutively, ending with row 2.

Row 107: Ch 1, sc in each st across, fasten off.

Row 108: Working in starting ch on opposite side of row 1, join jade with sc in first ch, sc in each ch across, fasten off.

WHITE STRIP (make 3)

Reversing colors, work same as Jade Strip.

To **join Strips,** starting with Jade Strip, alternating Jade Strips and White Strips, matching ends of rows, hold two Strips side by side, join white with sl st in first row of first Strip, ch 2, sl st in first row of 2nd Strip, (ch 2, sl st in next row of first Strip, ch 2, sl st in next row of second Strip) across, fasten off. Repeat with remaining Strips.

FRINGE

For **each Fringe,** cut three strands each 12" long. With all three strands held together, fold in half, insert hook in st, draw fold through, draw all loose ends through fold, tighten, trim ends.

With white, Fringe in every other st on ends of Jade Strips and in joinings. With jade, Fringe in every other st on ends of White Strips.✣

Dapped Daisies

Designer: *Rosetta Harshman*

Size: 41½" x 60".

Materials: Worsted-weight yarn — 29 oz. off-white, 7 oz. each green and yellow; tapestry needle; G crochet hook or size needed to obtain gauge.

Gauge: 15 sts = 4"; Rnds 1-3 of Block = 2¾". Block is 9¼" square.

Skill Level: ★★ Average

INSTRUCTIONS

BLOCK (make 24)

Rnd 1: With yellow, ch 5, sl st in first ch to form ring, ch 3, 15 dc in ring, join with sl st in top of ch-3 (16 dc).

Rnd 2: Ch 1, 2 sc in each st around, join with sl st in first sc, fasten off (32 sc).

Rnd 3: Working this rnd in **back lps** only, join off-white with sl st in any st, ch 2, hdc in each of next 3 sts, ch 10, sl st in top of last hdc made, (hdc in next 4 sts, ch 10, sl st in top of last hdc made) around, join with sl st in top of ch-2 (32 hdc, 8 ch-10 lps).

Rnd 4: Sl st in next st, ch 1, sc in same st, *[skip next 2 sts, (7 dc, ch 3, 7 dc) in next ch lp, skip next st], sc in next st; repeat from * 6 more times; repeat between [ ], join with sl st in first sc, fasten off (8 petals).

NOTE: For **double treble crochet (dtr),** yo 3 times, insert hook in next st, yo, draw lp through, (yo, draw through 2 lps on hook) 4 times.

Rnd 5: Join green with sc in any ch-3 sp at tip of any petal, ch 5, dtr in next sc between petals, ch 5, (sc in ch-3 sp at tip of next petal, ch 5, dtr in next sc between petals, ch 5) around, join (8 sc, 8 dtr).

Rnd 6: Ch 1, sc in first st, (*ch 10, skip next dtr, sc in next sc, ch 7, dtr in next dtr, ch 7*, sc in next sc) 3 times; repeat between **, join (8 ch-7 sps, 8 sc, 4 ch-10 sps, 4 dtr).

Rnd 7: Ch 2, (*8 hdc in next ch-10 sp, hdc in next st, 6 hdc in next ch-7 sp, 3 hdc in next st, 6 hdc in next ch-7 sp*, hdc in next st) 3 times; repeat between **, join with sl st in top of ch-2, fasten off (100 hdc).

Rnd 8: Join off-white with sl st in center corner st of any corner, ch 3, (dc, ch 2, 2 dc) in same st, dc in each st around with (2 dc, ch 2, 2 dc) in each center corner st, join with sl st in top of ch-3, fasten off (112 dc, 4 ch-2 sps).

Rnd 9: Join green with sc in any corner ch-2 sp, (sc, ch 2, 2 sc) in same sp, sc in each st around with (2 sc, ch 2, 2 sc) in each corner ch-2 sp, join with sl st in first sc, fasten off (128 sc, 4 ch-2 sps).

Rnd 10: Join off-white with sl st in any corner ch-2 sp, ch 3, (dc, ch 2, 2 dc) in same sp, dc in each st around with (2 dc, ch 2, 2 dc) in each corner ch-2 sp, join with sl st in top of ch-3, fasten off (36 dc on each side between corner ch-2 sps).

Holding Blocks wrong sides togerther, matching sts, with off-white, sew together in four rows of six Blocks each.

BORDER

Rnd 1: Working around outer edge, join off-white with sl st in any corner ch sp, ch 3, (dc, ch 3, 2 dc) in same sp, dc in each st, in ch sp on each side of seams and in each seam around with (2 dc, ch 3, 2 dc) in each corner ch sp, join with sl st in top of ch-3, fasten off (157 dc on each short end between corner ch sps, 235 dc on each long edge between corner ch sps).

Rnd 2: Join green with sc in any corner ch sp, (sc, ch 3, 2 sc) in same sp, sc in each st around with (2 sc, ch 3, 2 sc) in each corner ch sp, join with sl st in first sc, fasten off (161 sc on each short end between corner ch sps, 239 sc on each long edge between corner ch sps).

Rnd 3: Join yellow with sl st in corner ch sp before one long edge, ch 3, 4 dc in same sp, dc in each st around with 5 dc in each corner ch sp, join with sl st in top of ch-3 (165 dc on each short end between corner dc, 243 dc on each long edge between corner dc).

Rnd 4: Ch 1, sc in first st, sc in next st, *ch 5, skip next 2 sts, sc in each of next 3 sts, (ch 5, skip next 4 sts, sc in each of next 3 sts) 34 times, ch 5, skip next 3 sts, sc in each of next 3 sts*; repeat between ( ) 23 more times; repeat between **; repeat between ( ) 22 more times, ch 5, skip next 4 sts, sc in last st, join with sl st in first sc.

Continued on page 40

Dew-Kissed Petals

Size: 47" x 73".

Materials: Worsted-weight yarn — 29 oz. white, 9½ oz. lt. green and 8½ oz. pink; I crochet hook or size needed to obtain gauge.

Gauge: 7 dc and 6 ch-2 sps = 5"; 7 dc rows = 5".

Skill Level: ★★★ Advanced

Designer: By Elizabeth Owens

INSTRUCTIONS

CENTER PANEL

Center Strip

Row 1: With white, ch 44, dc in 8th ch from hook, (ch 2, skip next 2 chs, dc in next ch) across, turn (14 dc, 13 ch-2 sps).

NOTES: For **beginning mesh (beg mesh),** ch 5, skip next ch sp, dc in next dc.

For **mesh,** ch 2, skip next 2 chs, dc in next dc or ch.

For **end mesh,** ch 2, dc in 3rd ch of ch-5.

Row 2: Beg mesh, mesh 11 times, end mesh, turn (13 mesh).

Row 3: Beg mesh, mesh 4 times, ch 3, skip next ch sp, dc in next ch sp, ch 3, skip next ch sp, dc in next dc, mesh 4 times, end mesh, turn.

Row 4: Beg mesh, mesh 3 times, ch 5, skip next 2 ch sps, 3 dc in next dc, ch 5, skip next 2 ch sps, dc in next dc, mesh 3 times, end mesh, turn.

Row 5: Beg mesh, mesh 3 times, ch 4, 2 dc in next dc, dc in next dc, 2 dc in next dc, ch 4, dc in next dc, mesh 3 times, end mesh, turn.

Row 6: Beg mesh, mesh 3 times, ch 3, 2 dc in next dc, dc in each of next 3 dc, 2 dc in next dc, ch 3, dc in next dc, mesh 3 times, end mesh, turn.

Row 7: Beg mesh, mesh 3 times, ch 7; to **tr next 7 dc tog,** *yo 2 times, insert hook in next dc, yo, draw lp through, (yo, draw through 2 lps on hook) 2 times; repeat from * 6 more times, yo, draw through all 8 lps on hook; ch 7, dc in next dc, mesh 3 times, end mesh, turn.

Row 8: Beg mesh, mesh 3 times, ch 7, sc in next st, ch 7, dc in next dc, mesh 3 times, end mesh, turn.

NOTES: For **cluster (cl),** yo 2 times, insert hook in next ch sp, yo, draw lp through, (yo, draw through 2 lps on hook) 2 times, *yo 2 times, insert hook in same sp, yo, draw lp through, (yo, draw through 2 lps on hook) 2 times; repeat from *, yo, draw through all 4 lps on hook.

For **right cluster (right cl),** ch 3, *yo 2 times, insert hook in top of last dc or sc made, yo, draw lp through, (yo, draw through 2 lps on hook) 2 times; repeat from *, yo, draw through all 3 lps on hook.

For **left cluster (left cl),** ch 4, yo 2 times, insert hook in 4th ch from hook, *yo, draw lp through, (yo, draw through 2 lps on hook) 2 times*, yo 2 times, insert hook in same ch; repeat between **, yo, draw through all 3 lps on hook.

Row 9: Beg mesh, mesh 3 times, right cl, ch 1, (cl in next ch sp, ch 1) 2 times, left cl, dc in next dc, mesh 3 times, end mesh, turn.

Row 10: Beg mesh, mesh 3 times, right cl, sc in base of next cl, ch 4, skip next 2 cls, sc in top of next cl, right cl, dc in next dc, mesh 3 times, end mesh, turn.

Row 11: Beg mesh, mesh 3 times, ch 4, (cl, ch 4, cl) in next ch sp, ch 4, dc in next dc, mesh 3 times, end mesh, turn.

Row 12: Beg mesh, mesh 3 times, ch 7, skip next ch sp, sc in next ch sp, ch 7, skip next ch sp, dc in next dc, mesh 3 times, end mesh, turn.

Row 13: Beg mesh, mesh 3 times, ch 3, 7 tr in next sc, ch 3, dc in next dc, mesh 3 times, end mesh, turn.

Row 14: Beg mesh, mesh 3 times, ch 4, dc next 2 dc tog, dc in each of next 3 dc, dc next 2 dc tog, ch 4, dc in next dc, mesh 3 times, end mesh, turn.

Row 15: Beg mesh, mesh 3 times, ch 5, dc next 2 dc tog, dc in next dc, dc next 2 dc tog, ch 5, dc in next dc, mesh 3 times, end mesh, turn.

Row 16: Beg mesh, mesh 3 times, ch 6, dc next 3 dc tog, ch 6, dc in next dc, mesh 3 times, end mesh, turn.

Row 17: Beg mesh, mesh 10 times, end mesh, turn.

Row 18: Beg mesh, mesh 4 times, ch 2, (dc in next ch sp, ch 2) 2 times, dc in next dc, mesh 4

Continued on page 40

Evening Glow

Size: 47" x 68½".

Materials: Worsted-weight yarn — 32 oz. spruce green, 24 oz. navy, 15 oz. lt. gold, 14 oz. each red and burgundy; H crochet hook or size needed to obtain gauge.

Gauge: Rnds 1-3 of Block = 4" across. Block is 10¾" square.

Skill Level: ★★★★ Challenging

Designer: Jennifer Christiansen McClain

INSTRUCTIONS

BLOCK (make 24)

Rnd 1: With lt. gold, ch 2, 8 sc in 2nd ch from hook, join with sl st in first sc (8 sc).

Rnd 2: Ch 1, sc first 2 sts tog, ch 3, (sc same st as last st and next st tog, ch 3) 6 times, sc same st as last st and first st worked tog, ch 3, join, fasten off (8 sc, 8 ch-3 sps).

NOTE: For **popcorn (pc),** 3 dc in next st, drop lp from hook, insert hook in first dc of 3-dc group, pick up dropped lp, draw through st.

Rnd 3: Join burgundy with sl st in any ch sp, ch 3, *[pc in next st, (2 dc, ch 2, 2 dc) in next ch sp, pc in next st], dc in next ch sp; repeat from * 2 more times; repeat between [ ], join with sl st in top of ch-3 (20 dc, 8 pc, 4 ch-2 sps).

Rnd 4: Ch 1, sc in first st, ch 3, skip next st, sc in next st, ch 3, skip next st, *[(sc, ch 3, sc) in next ch sp, ch 3, skip next st], (sc in next st, ch 3, skip next st) across to next corner ch sp; repeat from * 2 more times; repeat between [ ], sc in next st, ch 3, skip last st, join with sl st in first sc, fasten off (20 ch-3 sps).

Rnd 5: Working behind ch sps of last rnd into skipped sts on rnd before last, join green with sl st in first skipped st on rnd before last after any corner ch sp, ch 3, sl st in **back lp** of 2nd ch on corresponding ch-3 sp of last rnd, dc in same st on rnd before last, *dc in next skipped st on rnd before last, sl st in **back lp** of 2nd ch on corresponding ch-3 sp of last rnd, dc in same st on rnd before last) across to next corner ch sp; working in ch sp on rnd before last between sts of last rnd, dc in next ch sp, sl st in **back lp** of 2nd ch on corresponding ch-3 sp of last rnd, dc in same sp on rnd before last; repeat from * around, join with sl st in top of ch-3 (40 dc, 20 sl sts).

Rnd 6: Skipping all sl sts, ch 1, sc first 2 dc tog, ch 3, (sc next 2 dc tog, ch 3) 3 times, (sc in next dc, ch 3) 2 times, *(sc next 2 dc tog, ch 3) 4 times, (sc in next dc, ch 3) 2 times; repeat from * around, join with sl st in first sc (24 ch-3 sps).

Rnd 7: Sl st in first ch sp, ch 1, 2 sc in same sp, *[3 sc in next ch sp, 2 sc in each of next 2 ch sps, (2 dc, ch 2, 2 dc) in next ch sp], 2 sc in each of next 2 ch sps; repeat from * 2 more times; repeat between [ ], 2 sc in last ch sp, join (44 sc, 16 dc, 4 ch-2 sps).

Rnd 8: Sl st in next st, ch 1, sc in same st, *[ch 3, skip next st, (sc in next st, ch 3, skip next st) across] to next corner ch sp, (sc, ch 3, sc) in next ch sp; repeat from * 2 more times; repeat between [ ], join (36 sc, 36 ch-3 sps).

Rnd 9: Working behind ch sps of last rnd into skipped sts on rnd before last, join navy with sl st in first skipped st on rnd before last after any corner ch sp, ch 3, sl st in **back lp** of 2nd ch on corresponding ch-3 sp of last rnd, dc in same st on rnd before last, *(dc in next skipped st on rnd before last, sl st in **back lp** of 2nd ch on corresponding ch-3 sp of last rnd, dc in same st on rnd before last) across to next corner ch sp; working in ch sp on rnd before last between sts of last rnd, 2 dc in next ch sp, sl st in **back lp** of 2nd ch on corresponding ch-3 sp on last rnd, 2 dc in same sp on rnd before last; repeat from * around, join with sl st in top of ch-3 (80 dc, 36 sl sts).

Rnd 10: Skipping all sl sts, ch 1, (sc in each dc across to next corner sl st, ch 3, skip next sl st) 4 times; sc in each of last 2 dc, join with sl st in first sc (80 sc, 4 ch-3 sps).

Rnd 11: Ch 1, 2 sc in first st, skip next st, *(2 sc in next st, skip next st) across to next corner ch sp, (hdc, dc, ch 2, dc, hdc) in next ch sp, skip next 2 sts; repeat from * around, join (88 sts).

Rnd 12: Ch 1, sc in first st, ch 3, skip next st, *(sc in next st, ch 3, skip next st) across to next corner ch sp, (sc, ch 2, sc) in next ch sp, ch 3, skip next 2 sts; repeat from * around, join, fasten off (48 sc, 44 ch-3 sps, 4 ch-2 sps).

Rnd 13: Join lt. gold with sc in first st after any corner ch sp; working behind ch sps on last rnd into skipped sts on rnd before last, *[skip next

Continued on page 41

Climbing Roses

Designer: Rosetta Harshman

Size: 50" x 72".

Materials: Worsted-weight yarn — 48 oz. red, 29 oz. white and 18 oz. green; G crochet hook or size needed to obtain gauge.

Gauge: 4 dc = 1"; rnd 1 of Flower = 1½" across.

Skill Level: ★★ Average

INSTRUCTIONS

STRIP (make 7)

First Rose

Rnd 1: With red, ch 6, sl st in first ch to form ring, ch 6, (dc in ring, ch 3) 7 times, join with sl st in 3rd ch of ch-6 (8 dc, 8 ch-3 sps).

Rnd 2: Sl st in first ch sp, ch 1, (sc, 3 dc, sc) in same sp, (sc, 3 dc, sc) in each ch sp around, join with sl st in first sc (8 petals).

Rnd 3: Working behind last rnd, ch 3, sc around post of first dc on rnd 1, ch 8, (sc around post of next dc on rnd 1, ch 8) around, skip first ch-3, join with sl st in first sc (8 ch-8 lps).

Rnd 4: Sl st in first ch lp, ch 1, (sc, hdc, 5 dc, hdc, sc) in same lp, (sc, hdc, 5 dc, hdc, sc) in each ch lp around, join with sl st in first sc, fasten off.

Second Rose

Rnds 1-3: Repeat same rnds of First Rose.

Rnd 4: Sl st in first ch lp, ch 1, (sc, hdc, 5 dc, hdc, sc) in same lp, (sc, hdc, 5 dc, hdc, sc) in each of next 5 ch lps, (sc, hdc, 3 dc) in next ch lp, sl st in center dc of 4th petal on last Rose made, (2 dc, hdc, sc) in same lp on this Rose, (sc, hdc, 3 dc) in next ch lp, sl st in center dc of 3rd petal on last Rose made, (2 dc, hdc, sc) in same lp on this Rose, join with sl st in first sc, fasten off.

Repeat Second Rose 16 more times for a total of 18 Roses.

BORDER

Rnd 1: Working around outer edge of Roses, join green with sc in center dc of petal after joined petals on First Rose, [(ch 6, sc in center dc of next petal) 5 times, ch 4; for **treble decrease (tr dec),** yo 2 times, insert hook in 3rd st of next petal, yo, draw lp through, (yo, draw through 2 lps on hook) 2 times, yo 2 times, insert hook in 7th st of next petal, yo, draw lp through, (yo, draw through 2 lps on hook) 2 times, yo, draw through all 3 lps on hook; ch 4, *(sc in center dc of next petal, ch 4) 2 times, tr dec, ch 4; repeat from * 15 more times], sc in center dc of next petal; repeat between [ ], join with sl st in first sc (100 ch-4 sps, 10 ch-6 sps).

Rnd 2: Sl st in first ch sp, ch 3, 6 dc in same sp, 7 dc in each of next 4 ch sps, 5 dc in each of next 50 ch sps, 7 dc in each of next 5 ch sps, 5 dc in each of next 50 ch sps, join with sl st in top of ch-3, fasten off (570 dc).

Rnd 3: Join white with sl st in first st, ch 3, (dc in each st across to center st on end, 2 dc in next st) 2 times, dc in each st around, join (572).

Rnd 4: Ch 3; working over ch-3 just made, dc in last st on last rnd; for **cross stitch (cr st),** skip next st, dc in next st; working over dc just made, dc in skipped st; cr st around, join (286 cr sts).

Rnd 5: Ch 1, sc in each st around with 2 sc in center 22 sts on each end, join, fasten off.

To **join Strips,** holding two Strips wrong sides together, working through both thicknesses, with red, sc long edges together through **back lps** only, leaving center 44 sts on each end unworked, fasten off.

Repeat with remaining Strips.

EDGING

Rnd 1: Working around entire outer edge, join red with sc in 2nd st after any seam, (sc in each st around to 3 sts before next seam, sc next 2 sts tog, sc next st and first st on next Strip tog) around, join with sl st in first sc, fasten off.

NOTE: For **decrease (dec),** insert hook in next st, yo, draw lp through, skip next 3 sts, insert hook in next st, yo, draw lp through, yo, draw through all 3 lps on hook, ch 3, skip next st.

Rnd 2: Join green with sc in 4th st, ch 3, skip next st, (sc in next st, ch 3, skip next st) around with dec at each indentation, join, fasten off.✣

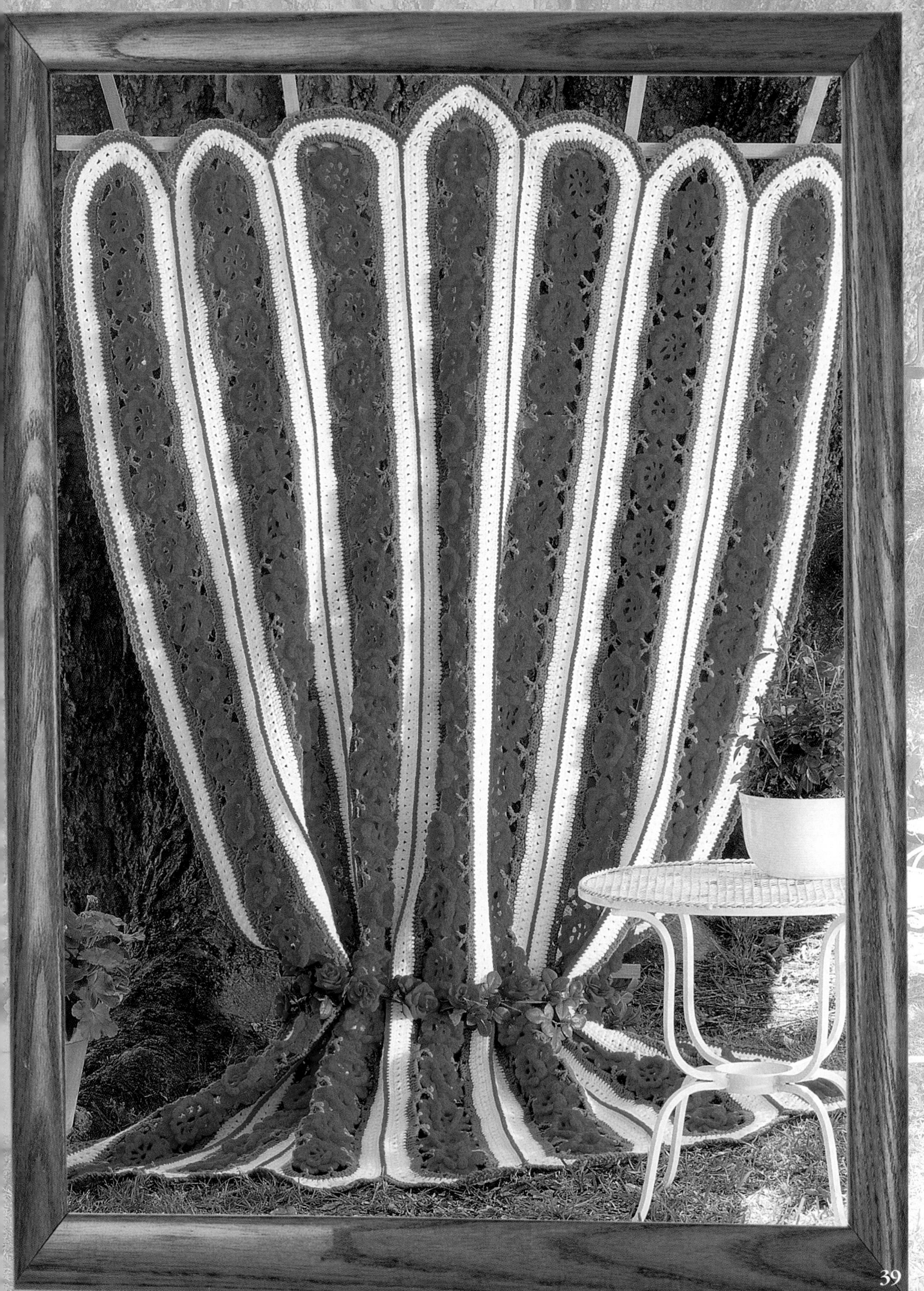

Dapped Daisies

continued from page 32

NOTE: For **picot,** ch 3, sc in 3rd ch from hook.

Rnd 5: Sl st in next st, sl st in next ch sp, ch 3, dc in same sp, ◊[(picot, 2 dc in same sp) 3 times, *2 dc in next ch sp, (picot, 2 dc in same sp) 2 times; repeat from * across] to next corner ch sp, 2 dc in next ch sp; repeat from ◊ 2 more times; repeat between [ ], join with sl st in top of ch-3, fasten off.✣

Dew-Kissed Petals

continued from page 35

times, end mesh, turn.

Rows 19-21: Beg mesh, mesh 11 times, end mesh, turn.

Rows 22-95: Repeat rows 3-21 consecutively, ending with row 19. At end of last row, fasten off.

Right Side Edging

Row 1: With right side of work facing you, working in ends of rows, join pink with sl st in first row, ch 4, 3 tr in same row, (*sc in top of dc on next row, 5 dc in top of dc on next row, sc in top of dc on next row*, skip next row, 7 tr around post of st on next row) across to last 4 rows; repeat between **, 4 tr in top of dc on last row, turn, fasten off (38 sc, 19 5-dc groups, 18 7-tr groups, 2 4-tr groups).

Row 2: Join white with sc in first st, *[ch 7; for **decrease (dec),** yo 2 times, insert hook in next sc, yo, draw lp through, (yo, draw through 2 lps on hook) 2 times, skip next 2 sts, yo, insert hook in next st, yo, draw lp through, yo, draw through 2 lps on hook, skip next 2 sts, yo 2 times, insert hook in next sc, yo, draw lp through, (yo, draw lp 2 lps on hook) 2 times, yo, draw through all 4 lps on hook; ch 7], sc in center st of next 7-tr group; repeat from * 17 more times; repeat between [ ], sc in last st, turn, fasten off.

Row 3: Join lt. green with sl st in first st, ch 4, 3 tr in same st, sc in next ch sp, 5 dc in next st, sc in next ch sp, (7 tr in next st, sc in next ch sp, 5 dc in next st, sc in next ch sp) across to last st, 4 tr in last st, turn, fasten off.

Row 4: Repeat row 2.

Left Edging

Row 1: With right side facing you, working in ends of rows, join pink with sl st in last row on Center Strip, ch 4, 3 tr in same row, (*sc in bottom of dc on next row, 5 dc in bottom of dc on next row, sc in bottom of dc on next row*, skip next row, 7 tr around post of st on next row) across to last 4 rows; repeat between **, 4 tr in bottom of dc on last row, turn, fasten off (38 sc, 19 5-dc groups, 18 7-tr groups, 2 4-tr groups).

Rows 2-4: Repeat same rows of Right Edging.

RIGHT PANEL

Center Strip

Work same as Center Strip on Center Panel.

Right Side Edging

Work same as Right Side Edging on Center Panel.

Left Side Edging

Rows 1-3: Repeat same rows of Left Side Edging on Center Panel.

Row 4: Join white with sc in first st; joining on to right side of Center Panel, ch 3, sc in first ch sp on Center Panel, ch 3, work dec on this Panel, ch 3, sc in next ch sp on Center Panel, ch 3, (sc in center st of next 7-tr group on this Panel, ch 3, sc in next ch sp on Center Panel, ch 3, work dec on this Panel, ch 3, sc in next ch sp on Center Panel, ch 3) across to last st on this Panel, sc in last st, fasten off.

LEFT PANEL

Center Strip

Work same as Center Strip on Center Panel.

Left Side Edging

Work same as Left Side Edging on Center Panel.

Right Side Edging

Rows 1-3: Repeat same rows of Right Side Edging on Center Panel.

Row 4: Joining on to left side of Center Panel, repeat same row of Left Side Edging on Right Panel.

TOP BORDER

Working in sts and in ends of rows across top of

Afghan, with right side facing you, join lt. green with sl st in top of first st on corner, ch 4, 6 tr in same st, *[sc in first dc on next Center Strip, (5 dc in next dc, sc in next dc) 2 times, 2 sc in next ch sp, sc in next dc, skip next ch sp, 7 tr in next ch sp, skip next ch sp, sc in next dc, 2 sc in next ch sp, (sc in next dc, 5 dc in next dc) 2 times, sc in last dc on this Strip, skip next tr row, 7 tr in next sc row], sc in top of next tr row, ch 5, skip next ch sp, sc in next joining sc, ch 5, skip next ch sp, sc in top of next tr row, 7 tr in next sc row; repeat from *; repeat between [ ], sl st in top of ch-4, fasten off.

BOTTOM BORDER

Working in sts and in ends of rows across bottom of Afghan, work same as Top Border.✣

Evening Glow

continued from page 36

skipped st on rnd before last, (dc in next skipped st on rnd before last, sc in next st on last rnd) across to next corner ch sp; working into ch sp on rnd before last between sts of last rnd, (dc, ch 2, dc) in next ch sp], sc in next st on last rnd; repeat from * 2 more times; repeat between [ ], join, fasten off (100 sts, 4 ch-2 sps).

Rnd 14: Join red with sc in first sc, hdc in next dc and in next ch-3 sp on rnd before last at same time, *sc in next sc, (hdc in next dc and in next ch-3 sp on rnd before last at same time, sc in next sc) across to dc before next corner ch sp, hdc in next dc and in next corner ch sp on rnd before last at same time, (sc, ch 2, sc) in corner ch sp on last rnd only, hdc in next dc and in same ch sp on rnd before last at same time; repeat from * around, join, fasten off (27 sts on each side between corner ch-2 sps).

Rnd 15: Join green with sc in any sc, sc in same st; skipping all hdc sts, 2 sc in each sc around with (2 sc, ch 2, 2 sc) in each corner ch sp, join, fasten off (30 sc on each side between corner ch-2 sps).

ASSEMBLY

Holding two Blocks right sides together, matching sts and working through both thicknesses, join green with sc in first corner ch sp, sc in each st across to next corner ch sp, sc in next ch sp, ch 1; holding two more Blocks right sides together, sc in first corner ch sp, sc in each st across to next corner ch sp, sc in next ch sp. Continue joining Blocks in same manner until 12 Blocks are joined in two strips of six Blocks each, fasten off. Repeat with remaining Blocks, making a total of four joined strips of six Blocks each. Working across strips, join remaining edges in same manner.

BORDER

Rnd 1: Working around outer edge, join green with sc in corner ch sp before one long edge, ch 2, sc in same sp, sc in each st, hdc in ch sps on each side of seams and hdc in each seam around with (sc, ch 2, sc) in each corner ch sp, join with sl st in first sc (131 sts on each short end between corner ch sps, 197 sts on each long edge between corner ch sps).

Rnd 2: Sl st in first ch sp, ch 1, (sc, ch 3, sc) in same sp, *[ch 3, skip next st, (sc in next st, ch 3, skip next st) across] to next corner ch sp, (sc, ch 3, sc) in next ch sp; repeat from * 2 more times; repeat between [ ], join, fasten off.

Rnd 3: With navy, repeat rnd 5 of Block.

Rnd 4: Join lt. gold with sc in first dc after corner sl st, skipping all sl sts, *[ch 2, (sc next 2 dc tog, ch 2) across to dc before next corner sl st, sc in next dc, ch 3, skip next sl st], sc in next dc; repeat from * 2 more times; repeat between [ ], join with sl st in first sc, fasten off.

Rnd 5: Join burgundy with sc in any ch-2 sp, ch 3, sc in same sp, (sc, ch 3, sc) in each ch-2 sp around with (sc, ch 3, sc, ch 5, sc, ch 3, sc) in each corner ch-3 sp, join, fasten off.✣

Photo by Mary Van de Ven, Hawaii

Rainbow in the Sky

"My heart leaps up when I behold
A rainbow in the sky:
So was it when my life began;
So is it now I am a man; . . ."

—William Wordsworth

Beginning Reflections

Designer: *Wendy J. Bennett*

Size: 35" x 40".

Materials: Sport-weight yarn — 12 oz. cream, 8 oz. each med. blue and pink, 4 oz. each purple and dk. blue; J crochet hook or size needed to obtain gauge.

Gauge: 7 sts = 3"; 7 pattern rows = 4".

Note: Entire pattern is worked holding 2 strands yarn together.

Skill Level: ★★Average

INSTRUCTIONS

AFGHAN

Row 1: With 2 strands cream, ch 94, sc in 2nd ch from hook, dc in next ch, tr in next ch, (sc in next ch, dc in next ch, tr in next ch) across, turn (93 sts).

Rows 2-6: Ch 1, sc in first st, dc in next st, tr in next st, (sc in next st, dc in next st, tr in next st) across, turn. At end of last row, fasten off.

Row 7: With one strand each cream and med. blue, join with sc in first st, dc in next st, tr in next st, (sc in next st, dc in next st, tr in next st) across, turn.

Rows 8-9: Repeat row 2. At end of last row, fasten off.

Rows 10-30: Working in color sequence of med. blue, med. blue/dk. blue, dk. blue, med. blue/dk. blue, med. blue, cream/med. blue, cream, repeat rows 7-9 consecutively. At end of last row, **do not** fasten off.

Rows 31-33: Repeat row 2. At end of last row, fasten off.

Rows 34-57: Working in color sequence of cream/pink, pink, pink/purple, purple, pink/purple, pink, cream/pink, cream, repeat rows 7-9 consecutively. At end of last row, **do not** fasten off.

Rows 58-60: Repeat row 2. At end of last row, fasten off.✣

Welch's
NON-ALCOHOLIC
SPARKLING
RED

Colorful Promises

Designer: Sue Childress

Size: 53" x 62½".

Materials: Worsted-weight yarn — 12 oz. cream, 8 oz. lt. green, 4 oz. each lt. pink, dk. pink, lt. yellow, dk. yellow, lt. peach, dk. peach, lt. purple, dk. purple, lt. aqua, dk. aqua, lt. blue and dk. blue; G crochet hook or size needed to obtain gauge.

Gauge: Rnds 1-3 = 3" across. Each Block is 9" square before joining.

Skill Level: ★★ Average

INSTRUCTIONS

BLOCK (make 5 of each color combination, see Note)

NOTE: Color combinations for Blocks are lt. pink/dk. pink, lt. yellow/dk. yellow, lt. peach/dk. peach, lt. purple/dk. purple, lt. aqua/dk. aqua and lt. blue/dk. blue.

Rnd 1: With lt. color, ch 4, 11 dc in 4th ch from hook, join with sl st in top of ch-3 (12 dc).

NOTE: For **popcorn (pc),** 4 dc in next st, drop lp from hook, insert hook in first st of 4-dc group, draw dropped lp through, ch 1.

Rnd 2: Ch 1, sc in first st, pc in next st, (sc in next st, pc in next st) around, join with sl st in first sc (6 pc, 6 sc).

Rnd 3: Ch 3, 2 dc in same st, ch 2, sc in top of next pc, ch 2, (3 dc in next sc, ch 2, sc in top of next pc, ch 2) around, join with sl st in top of ch-3, fasten off (18 dc, 12 ch-2 sps).

NOTE: For **beginning popcorn (beg pc),** ch 3, 3 dc in same st, drop lp from hook, insert hook in top of ch-3, draw dropped lp through, ch 1.

Rnd 4: Join dk. color with sl st in first ch-2 sp, beg pc, pc in next ch-2 sp, 5 dc in center st of next 3-dc group, (pc in each of next 2 ch-2 sps, 5 dc in center st of next 3-dc group) around, join with sl st in top of beg pc, fasten off (30 dc, 12 pc).

Rnd 5: Join lt. green with sl st in sp between first 2 pc, beg pc, *[ch 1, pc in next dc, (ch 1, skip next dc, pc in next dc) 2 times, ch 1], pc in sp between next 2 pc; repeat from * 4 more times; repeat between [ ], join, fasten off (24 pc, 24 ch sps).

Rnd 6: Join cream with sl st in 4th ch sp, ch 3, (2 dc, ch 2, 3 dc) in same sp, 3 dc in each of next 5 ch sps, *(3 dc, ch 2, 3 dc) in next ch sp, 3 dc in each of next 5 ch sps; repeat from * around, join with sl st in top of ch-3 (84 dc, 4 ch sps).

NOTES: For **beginning shell (beg shell),** ch 3, (dc, ch 2, 2 dc) in same ch sp.

For **shell,** (2 dc, ch 2, 2 dc) in next ch sp.

Rnd 7: Sl st in each of next 2 sts, sl st in next ch sp, beg shell, (*skip next 3 sts, dc in next 15 sts, skip next 3 sts*, shell in next ch sp) 3 times; repeat between **, join, fasten off (60 dc, 4 shells).

Rnd 8: Join lt. color with sl st in any corner ch sp, beg shell, dc in each st around with shell in each corner ch sp, join, fasten off (76 dc, 4 shells).

Rnd 9: With dk. color, repeat rnd 8 (92 dc, 4 shells).

ASSEMBLY

Strip

To **join Blocks,** working in color sequence according to Assembly Diagram, holding 2 Blocks right sides together, matching sts, join lt. green with sc in corner ch sp on first Block, ch 2, pc in corresponding corner ch sp on Second Block, (*ch 1, skip next 2 sts on first Block, sc in next st, ch 1, skip next 2 sts on second Block, sc in next st, ch 1, skip next 2 sts on first Block, pc in next st, ch 1, skip next 2 sts on second Block, sc in next st*, ch 1, skip next 2 sts on first Block, sc in next st, ch 1, skip next 2 sts on second Block, pc in next st) 2 times; repeat between **, ch 1, sc in next corner ch sp on first Block, ch 1, pc in next corner ch sp on second Block, fasten off.

Continue to join Blocks in five strips of six Blocks each.

Join strips in same manner as Blocks with (ch 1, sc, ch 1) in each joining between Blocks.

BORDER

Rnd 1: Working around entire outer edge of Afghan, with right side facing you, join lt. green with sl st in any corner ch sp, beg shell, dc in each st, dc in each ch sp on each side of seams and 3 dc in each seam around with shell in each

Continued on page 58

After the Rain

Designer: Katherine Eng

for Monsanto's Designs for America Program

Size: Afghan is 40½" x 58½" not including Fringe.

Materials: Worsted-weight yarn — 16 oz. red, 11 oz. blue, 7 oz. lavender and 5 oz. magenta; G crochet hook or size needed to obtain gauge.

Gauge: 7 sc sts = 2"; 3 sc rows and one shell row = 1½". Each Panel is 6¾" wide.

Note: Leave 8" long tail at beginning and end of each row to be worked into Fringe.

Skill Level: ★★ Average

INSTRUCTIONS

FIRST PANEL

Row 1: For **first side,** with red, ch 220, sc in 2nd ch from hook, sc in each ch across, turn, fasten off (219 sc).

Row 2: Join magenta with sc in first st, *ch 1, skip next st, sc in next st; repeat from across, turn, fasten off (110 sc, 109 ch sps).

Row 3: Join red with sc in first st, sc in each ch sp and in each st across, **do not** turn, fasten off (219 sc).

NOTE: For **shell,** (2 dc, ch 2, 2 dc) in next st.

Row 4: Join blue with sc in first st, *sc in next st, skip next 2 sts, shell in next st, skip next 2 sts; repeat from * across to last 2 sts, sc in each of last 2 sts, turn, fasten off (39 sc, 36 shells).

Row 5: Join lavender with sl st in first st, ch 3, dc in same st, ch 2, sc in ch sp of next shell, ch 2, *dc in next sc, ch 2, sc in ch sp of next shell, ch 2; repeat from * across to last 2 sc, skip next sc, 2 dc in last sc, turn, fasten off (72 ch-2 sps, 39 dc, 36 sc).

Row 6: Join red with sc in first st, sc in each st and 2 sc in each ch-2 sp across, turn, fasten off (219 sc).

Row 7: Join magenta with sc in first st, *ch 1, skip next st, sc in next st; repeat from across, turn, fasten off (110 sc, 109 ch sps).

Row 8: Join red with sc in first st, sc in each ch sp and in each st across, **do not** turn, fasten off (219 sc).

Row 9: Join blue with sc in first st, *sc in next st, skip next 2 sts, shell in next st, skip next 2 sts; repeat from * across to last 2 sts, sc in each of last 2 sts, turn, fasten off (39 sc, 36 shells).

Row 10: Join lavender with sc in first sc, ch 3, sc in same st, sl st in next sc, *ch 3, (sl st, ch 3, sl st) in next shell, ch 3, sl st in next sc; repeat from * across to last sc, (sc, ch 3, sc) in last sc, **do not** turn, fasten off.

Row 11: For **2nd side,** working in starting ch on opposite side of row 1, join red with sc in first ch, sc in each ch across, turn, fasten off (219 sc).

Rows 12-20: Repeat rows 2-10.

SECOND PANEL

Rows 1-19: Repeat same rows of First Panel.

Row 20: To **join,** holding this and last Panels side by side, with right sides facing you, join lavender with sc in first sc, ch 1, sl st in corresponding ch-3 sp on previous Panel, ch 1, sc in same st on this Panel, sl st in next sc, *ch 3, sl st in next shell, ch 1, sl st in corresponding ch-3 sp on previous Panel, ch 1, sl st in same shell on this Panel, ch 3, sl st in next sc; repeat from * across to last sc, sc in last sc, ch 1, sl st in corresponding ch-3 sp on previous Panel, ch 1, sc in same sc on this Panel, fasten off.

NEXT PANELS

Repeat Second Panel four more times for a total of six Panels.

Continued on page 59

Jeweled Sky

Designer: Darla J. Fanton

Size: 50" x 67".

Materials: Worsted-weight yarn — 28 oz. white, 18 oz. assorted jewel tones; K crochet hook or size needed to obtain gauge.

Gauge: 4 bobbles = 5" long; Strip is 2¾" wide.

Notes: Each Strip requires approximately 1 oz. bobble color.

Skill Level: ★★ Average

INSTRUCTIONS

FIRST STRIP

Center

Row 1: With desired jewel color, ch 5; for **bobble,** *yo 3 times, insert hook in 5th ch from hook, yo, draw lp through, (yo, draw through 2 lps on hook) 3 times; repeat from * 4 more times in same ch, yo, draw through all 6 lps on hook, **do not** turn (1 bobble).

Rows 2-52: Ch 5, bobble in top of bobble, **do not** turn, ending with one Strip 52 bobbles long. At end of last row, fasten off.

Edging

Rnd 1: Working around outer edge and being careful not to twist bobbles, with right side facing you, join white with sc in base of first bobble, ch 6, (sc in base of next bobble, ch 6) across, sc in top of last bobble, ch 6, (sc in base of next bobble, ch 6) across, join with sl st in first sc (104 ch sps).

Rnd 2: Sl st in next ch sp, ch 1, (sc, hdc, dc, ch 3, dc, hdc, sc) in same sp and in next 51 ch sps, ch 5, (sc, hdc, dc, ch 3, dc, hdc, sc) in last 52 ch sps, **do not** join, fasten off.

SECOND STRIP

Center

Work same as First Strip Center.

Edging

Rnd 1: Work same rnd as First Strip Edging.

Rnd 2: Holding this Strip and previous Strip together, sl st in next ch sp, ch 1, (sc, hdc, dc) in same sp, ch 1, sl st in corresponding ch sp on previous Strip, ch 1. (dc, hdc, sc) in same ch sp on this Strip, *(sc, hdc, dc) in next ch-3 sp, ch 1, sl st in corresponding ch sp on previous Strip, ch 1, (dc, hdc, sc) in same ch sp on this Strip; repeat from * 50 more times, ch 5, (sc, hdc, dc, ch 3, dc, hdc, sc) in last 52 ch sps, **do not** join, fasten off.

Repeat Second Strip 16 more times for a total of 18 Strips. At end of last Strip, **do not** fasten off.

BORDER

Row 1: Working across ends of Strips, in worked ch-6 sps of rnd 2 on Edging, (sc, hdc, dc) in same sp, ch 3, (dc, hdc, sc) in next ch-6 sp on same Strip, *ch 8, (sc, hdc, dc) in next ch-6 sp on next Strip, ch 3, (dc, hdc, sc) in next ch-6 sp on same Strip; repeat from * across, sl st in next sc on Edging, fasten off.

Row 2: With right side facing you, working over ch-6 sps on opposite end of Strips, join white with sc in first ch-6 sp, (hdc, dc) in same sp, ch 3, (dc, hdc, sc) in next ch-6 sp on same Strip, *ch 8, (sc, hdc, dc) in next ch-6 sp on next Strip, ch 3, (dc, hdc, sc) in next ch-6 sp on same Strip; repeat from * across, sl st in next sc on Edging, fasten off.✣

Evening Shadows

Designer: Fran Hetchler

Size: 49" x 63".

Materials: Worsted-weight yarn — 16 oz. each black, purple and white, 8 oz. teal; H crochet hook or size needed to obtain gauge.

Gauge: 16 sts = 5"; 5 dc rows and 5 sc rows = 4".

Skill Level: ★★ Average

INSTRUCTIONS

AFGHAN

Row 1: With black, ch 153, dc in 4th ch from hook, dc in each ch across, turn (151 dc).

Row 2: Ch 3, dc in each st across, turn, fasten off.

NOTE: For **front post (fp,** see figure 9, page 159), yo, insert hook from front to back around post of corresponding st on row before last, yo, draw lp through, (yo, draw through 2 lps on hook) 2 times, skip next st on last row.

Row 3: Join purple with sc in first st, sc in next 4 sts, fp, (sc in next 9 sts, fp) across to last 5 sts, sc in last 5 sts, turn (136 sc, 15 fp).

Row 4: Ch 3, dc in each st across, turn, fasten off (151 dc).

Row 5: Join white with sc in first st, sc in next 4 sts, fp around next fp, (sc in next 9 sts, fp around next fp) across to last 5 sts, sc in last 5 sts, turn.

Rows 6-12: Working in color sequence of teal, white, purple, repeat rows 4 and 5 alternately, ending with row 4.

Row 13: Join black with sl st in first st, ch 3, dc in each st across, turn.

Rows 14-146: Repeat rows 2-13 consecutively, ending with row 2.

BORDER

Rnd 1: Working around outer edge, join white with sc in first st, 4 sc in same st, sc in each st, sc in end of each sc row and 2 sc in end of each dc row around with 5 sc in each corner st, join with sl st in first sc, fasten off.

Rnd 2: Working this rnd in **back lps** only, join teal with sc in center st of any 5-sc corner group, 2 sc in same st, sc in each st around with 3 sc in center st of each 5-sc corner group, join, fasten off.

Rnd 3: Working this rnd in **back lps** only, join purple with sc in any center corner st, 2 sc in same st, sc in each st around with 3 sc in each center corner st, join, fasten off.

Rnd 4: With black, repeat rnd 2.✣

Cascading Light

Designer: Jennifer Christiansen McClain

Size: 53" x 65" not including Fringe.

Materials: Worsted-weight yarn — 15 oz. off-white, 7 oz. dk. blue, 6 oz. each lt. blue, burgundy and dk. green, 5 oz. each rose and lt. green; I crochet hook or size needed to obtain gauge.

Gauge: 3 dc = 1; 2 dc rows = 1.

Skill Level: ★★ Average

INSTRUCTIONS

PANEL (make 4 using lt./dk. blue, 3 each using lt./dk. green and pink/burgundy for a total of 10 Panels)

Foundation

With dk. color, ch 4, dc in 4th ch from hook, (turn; ch 3, dc in top of last dc made) 60 more times; at end of last dc, **do not** turn or fasten off (62 lps).

First Edging

Row 1: Working along one edge of Foundation, ch 1, 3 sc in each lp across, **do not** turn, fasten off.

Row 2: Join lt. color with sl st in first st, ch 3, skip next st, dc in next st, ch 1; working back over dc just made, dc in joining sl st, (skip next 2 sts, dc in next st, ch 1; working back over last dc made, dc in first skipped st) across, dc in same st as last dc, **do not** turn, fasten off.

Row 3: Join lt. color with sc in top of ch-3, ch 2, skip next st and next ch-1 sp, sc next 2 sts tog, (ch 2, skip next ch-1 sp, sc next 2 sts tog) across, ch 2, skip next ch-1 sp, skip next st, sc in last st, **do not** turn, fasten off.

Row 4: Join dk. color with sc in first ch-2 sp, 2 sc in same sp, 3 sc in each ch-2 sp across, **do not** turn, fasten off.

Row 5: Join off-white with sc in first st, sc in each st across, fasten off.

Second Edging

Row 1: Working on opposite side of Panel, join dk. color with sc in first lp, 2 sc in same lp, 3 sc in each lp across, **do not** turn, fasten off.

Rows 2-5: Repeat same rows of First Edging.

ASSEMBLY

Hold one blue Panel and one burgundy Panel wrong sides together and with burgundy Panel facing you; join off-white with sc in first st of Edging on burgundy Panel, ch 1, sc in first st of Edging on blue Panel, (ch 1, skip next st on burgundy Panel, sc in next st, ch 1, skip next st on blue Panel, sc in next st) across, fasten off.

Beginning on opposite side of burgundy Panel and working in color sequence of green, blue, burgundy, green, blue, burgundy, green and blue, continue joining remaining Panels in same manner.

FRINGE

For **each Fringe,** cut 3 strands off-white each 14" long. With all 3 strands held together, fold in half, insert hook in row, draw fold through, draw all loose ends through fold, tighten. Trim ends.

Work eight Fringe evenly spaced across ends of rows on each Panel with two Fringe in each joining and one on each outer edge.✣

THE TALE OF PETER RABBIT

Gentle Dreams

Designer: *Vicky L. Tignanelli*

Size: 36" x 40".

Materials: Sport-weight yarn — 10 oz. white, 2 oz. each baby blue, royal blue, pink, rose, lilac, purple, baby green and med. green; tapestry needle; G crochet hook or size needed to obtain gauge.

Gauge: 4 sts = 1"; 10 post st rows = 3".

Skill Level: ★★ Average

INSTRUCTIONS

SQUARE (make one white; make 3 of each color)

Row 1: Ch 25, dc in 4th ch from hook, dc in each ch across, turn (23 dc).

NOTES: For **front post (fp,** see figure 9, page 159), yo, insert hook from front to back around post of next st, yo, draw lp through, (yo, draw through 2 lps on hook) 2 times.

For **back post (bp),** yo, insert hook from back to front around post of next st, yo, draw lp through, (yo, draw through 2 lps on hook) 2 times.

Ch-2 at beginning of each row counts as first hdc.

Rows 2-3: Ch 2, fp around each of next 3 sts, (bp around each of next 3 sts, fp around each of next 3 sts) across to last st, hdc in last st, turn.

Rows 4-5: Ch 2, bp around each of next 3 sts, (fp around each of next 3 sts, bp around each of next 3 sts) across to last st, hdc in last st, turn.

Rows 6-15: Repeat rows 2-5 consecutively, ending with row 3. At end of last row, fasten off.

Rnd 16: For **edging,** working around outer edge, with right side facing you, join white with sl st in first st on last row, ch 3, 2 dc in same st, dc in each st across with 3 dc in last hdc, evenly space 21 dc across ends of rows; working in starting ch on opposite side of row 1, 3 dc in first ch, dc in each ch across with 3 dc in last ch, evenly space 21 dc across ends of rows, join with sl st in top of ch-3 (96 dc).

Rnd 17: Ch 2, *[2 hdc in next st, hdc in next st, fp around next st, (bp around next st, fp around next st) 10 times], hdc in next st; repeat from * 2 more times; repeat between [ ], join with sl st in top of ch-2 (100 sts).

Rnd 18: Ch 2, 2 hdc in each of next 2 sts, (hdc in each st across to next 2-hdc corner, 2 hdc in each of next 2 sts) 3 times, hdc in each st across, join, fasten off (108 hdc).

NOTES: Refer to Assembly Diagram for suggested color placement.

Holding Squares wrong sides together, matching sts, sew five Squares together through **back lps** across one side. Repeat for a total of five Strips of five Squares each.

STRIP EDGING

Working around outer edge of strip, join white with sl st in first st after 4-hdc corner before one long edge (see Assembly Diagram), ch 2, *(hdc in each st across to last 2 sts before next seam, dc in each of next 2 sts, dc in next seam, dc in each of next 2 sts) across to last Square, (hdc in each st across to next 4-hdc corner, dc in next st, 2 dc in each of next 2 sts, dc in next st) 2 times*; working on opposite long edge of Strip; repeat between **, join with sl st in top of ch-2, fasten off.

NOTES: Join Strips according to Assembly Diagram.

Holding two Strips wrong sides together, matching sts, sew Strips together through **back lps** across one long edge. Repeat until all Strips are joined.

BORDER

Working around entire outer edge of Afghan, join white with sc in any st, ch 2, sl st in 2nd ch from hook, ch 1, skip next st, (sc in next st, ch 2, sl st in 2nd ch from hook, ch 1, skip next st) around skipping last one or 2 sts as needed, join with sl st in first sc, fasten off.✣

ASSEMBLY DIAGRAM

- ■ = Med. Green
- ■ = Baby Blue
- ■ = Royal Blue
- ■ = Lilac
- ■ = Purple
- ■ = Baby Green
- ■ = Rose
- ■ = Pink
- □ = White

Colorful Promises

continued from page 46

corner ch sp, join with sl st in top of ch-3, fasten off (159 dc across each short end between corner ch sps, 191 dc on each long edge between corner ch sps).

Rnd 2: Join dk. pink with sl st in corner ch sp before one long edge, beg shell, *[skip next st, (pc in next st, skip next st) across to next corner ch sp, shell in next ch sp, skip next st, (pc in next st, skip next st) across] to next corner ch sp changing to lt. pink in last st made (see figure 12, page 159), shell in next corner ch sp; repeat between [ ], join, fasten off.

Rnd 3: Join dk. purple with sl st in any corner ch sp, ch 3, (2 dc, ch 2, 3 dc) in same sp, ch 1; working in spaces between pc, (2 dc, ch 1) in each sp around with (3 dc, ch 2, 3 dc, ch 1) in each corner ch sp, join, fasten off.

Rnd 4: Join lt. purple with sl st in any corner ch-2 sp, ch 3, (2 dc, ch 2, 3 dc) in same sp, ch 1, (2 dc, ch 1) in each ch-1 sp around with (3 dc, ch 2, 3 dc, ch 1) in each corner ch sp, join, fasten off.

Rnds 5-7: Working in color sequence of dk. yellow, lt. yellow, dk. aqua, repeat rnd 4.✣

ASSEMBLY DIAGRAM

After the Rain

continued from page 49

FRINGE

For **each Fringe,** cut 16" yarn strands. Matching row colors, cut 2 strands yarn for each sc row and cut 3 strands yarn for each dc row. Holding all strands together, fold in half, insert hook in row, draw fold through, draw all loose ends through fold, tighten. Trim ends.

Fringe in end of each row on each end of Afghan.✣

Beautiful Things
"I love all beauteous things,
I seek and adore them;
God hath no better praise,
And man in his hasty days
Is honored for them. . . ."
—Robert Bridges

Crystal Treasure

Designer: Jennifer Christiansen McClain

Size: 52" x 61" not including Fringe.

Materials: Worsted-weight yarn — 50 oz. white, 11 oz. med. pink, 7 oz. green and 2½ oz. dk. pink; tapestry needle; G and H crochet hooks or sizes needed to obtain gauges.

Gauges: **G hook,** 2 sc and 2 V-sts = 2¼"; 3 sc rows and 2 V-st rows in pattern = 2¼". **H hook,** Block is 6" square.

Skill Level: ★★ Average

INSTRUCTIONS

STRIP (make 4)

Block (make 10)

NOTE: Use H hook for entire Block.

Rnd 1: With dk. pink, ch 2, 8 sc in 2nd ch from hook, join with sl st in first sc (8 sc).

Rnd 2: Ch 1, sc in first st, ch 2, (sc in next st, ch 2) around, join, fasten off (8 ch-2 sps).

NOTES: For **beginning cluster (beg cl),** ch 2, (yo, insert hook in same sp, yo, draw lp through, yo, draw through 2 lps on hook) 3 times, yo, draw through all 4 lps on hook.

For **cluster (cl),** yo, insert hook in next ch sp, yo, draw lp through, yo, draw through 2 lps on hook, (yo, insert hook in same sp, yo, draw lp through, yo, draw through 2 lps on hook) 3 times, yo, draw through all 5 lps on hook.

For **puff stitch (puff st),** yo, insert hook in ch sp, yo, draw up ⅝" long lp, (yo, insert hook in same sp, yo, draw up ⅝" long lp) 2 times, yo, draw through all 7 lps on hook.

Rnd 3: Join med. pink with sl st in any ch sp, beg cl, ch 3, (cl in next ch sp, ch 3) around, join with sl st in beg cl, fasten off (8 cls, 8 ch-3 sps).

Rnd 4: Join green with sl st in any ch sp, ch 1, (puff st, ch 2, puff st) in same sp, ch 3, *(puff st, ch 2, puff st) in next ch sp, ch 3; repeat from * around, join with sl st in first puff st, fasten off (16 puff sts, 8 ch-3 sps, 8 ch-2 sps).

Rnd 5: Join white with sc in any ch-2 sp, *[ch 1; working over next ch-3 sp, 3 dc in next cl on rnd before last, ch 1, sc in next ch-2 sp on last rnd, ch 1; working over next ch-3 sp, (3 tr, ch 2, 3 tr) in next cl on rnd before last, ch 1], sc in next ch-2 sp on last rnd; repeat from * 2 more times; repeat between [ ], join with sl st in first sc (24 tr, 16 ch-1 sps, 12 dc, 8 sc, 4 ch-2 sps).

Rnd 6: Sl st in first ch-1 sp, ch 1, sc in same sp, ch 1, *[skip next st, sc in next st, ch 1, (sc in next ch-1 sp, ch 1) 2 times, skip next st, sc in next st, ch 1, skip next st, (sc, ch 2, sc) in next corner ch-2 sp, ch 1, skip next st, sc in next st, ch 1, skip next st], (sc in next ch-1 sp, ch 1) 2 times; repeat from * 2 more times; repeat between [ ], sc in last ch-1 sp, ch 1, join (32 ch-1 sps, 4 ch-2 sps).

Rnd 7: Sl st in first ch-1 sp, ch 1, 2 sc in same sp, 2 sc in each ch-1 sp and 3 sc in each corner ch-2 sp around, join, fasten off (76 sc).

Placing Blocks together side to side to form Strip, with white, sew together across 20 sts (from center st of one corner to center st of other corner).

Border

NOTE: Use G hook for entire Border.

Row 1: Working across one long edge of Strip, join white with sc in first center corner st, (sc in each st across to next joined corner st before seam, hdc in joined corner st, dc in seam, hdc in next joined corner st after seam) across to last Block, sc in each st across ending in center corner st, turn (209 sts).

Row 2: Working this row in **back lps** only, ch 1, sl st in each st across, turn.

NOTES: For **beginning V-stitch (beg V-st),** ch 4, dc in same st.

For **V-stitch (V-st),** (dc, ch 1, dc) in next st or ch sp.

Row 3: Working in **remaining lps** of row 1, ch 1, sc in first st, (skip next st, V-st in next st, skip next st, sc in next st) across, turn (53 sc, 52 V-sts).

Row 4: Working this row in **front lps** only, beg V-st, (sc in ch sp of next V-st, V-st in next sc) across, turn (53 V-sts, 52 sc).

Row 5: Working this row in **back lps** only, sl

Continued on page 76

Imperial Jade

Designer: Katherine Eng

for Monsanto's Designs for America Program

Size: 44" x 66½".

Materials: Fuzzy worsted-weight yarn — 22 oz. med. green, 21 oz. dk. green and 12½ oz. dk. pink; tapestry needle; H crochet hook or size needed to obtain gauge.

Gauge: Block Center is 3¾" square. Each Block is 7½" square.

Skill Level: ★★ Average

INSTRUCTIONS

BLOCK (make 40)

Center

Rnd 1: With dk. pink, ch 4, sl st in first ch to form ring, ch 1, 8 sc in ring, join with sl st in first sc (8 sc).

Rnd 2: Ch 1, sc in first st, (2 dc, ch 2, 2 dc) in next st, *sc in next st, (2 dc, ch 2, 2 dc) in next st; repeat from * around, join, fasten off (16 dc, 4 sc, 4 ch-2 sps).

Rnd 3: Join med. green with sc in any ch-2 sp, *[ch 1, skip next 2 sts, (3 dc, ch 2, 3 dc) in next st, ch 1, skip next 2 sts], sc in next ch-2 sp; repeat from * 2 more times; repeat between [ ], join (24 dc, 8 ch-1 sps, 4 sc, 4 ch-2 sps).

Rnd 4: Ch 1, sc in each st and in each ch-1 sp around with (sc, ch 2, sc) in each corner ch-2 sp, join, fasten off (44 sc, 4 ch-2 sps).

First Rectangle

Row 1: Join dk. green with sc in top right corner ch-2 sp (see Assembly Diagram on page 77), ch 1, skip next st, (sc in next st, ch 1, skip next st) 5 times, sc in next ch-2 sp leaving remaining sts unworked, turn (7 sc, 6 ch-1 sps).

Rows 2-5: Ch 1, sc in first st, (ch 1, skip next ch-1 sp, sc in next st) across, turn. At end of last row, **do not** turn, fasten off.

Second Rectangle

Row 1: Join dk. green with sc in next unworked ch-2 sp on rnd 4 of Center (see Assembly Diagram), ch 1, skip next st, (sc in next st, ch 1, skip next st) 5 times, sc in next ch-2 sp leaving remaining sts unworked, turn (7 sc, 6 ch-1 sps).

Rows 2-5: Repeat same rows of First Rectangle.

First Corner

Row 1: Working in ends of rows across First Rectangle (see Assembly Diagram), join med. green with sc in row 1, (ch 1, skip next row, sc in next row) 2 times, turn (3 sc, 2 ch-1 sps).

Rows 2-5: Repeat same rows of First Rectangle.

Third Rectangle

Row 1: Join dk. green with sc in bottom right corner ch-2 sp on rnd 4 of Center (see Assembly Diagram), ch 1, skip next st, (sc in next st, ch 1, skip next st) 5 times, sc in next ch-2 sp, sl st in row 1 of adjoining piece, turn (7 sc, 6 ch-1 sps).

Row 2: Ch 1, sc in first sc, (ch 1, skip next ch-1 sp, sc in next st) across, turn.

Row 3: Ch 1, sc in first st, (ch 1, skip next ch-1 sp, sc in next st) across, skip next row on adjoining Piece, sl st in next row, turn.

Rows 4-5: Repeat rows 2 and 3. At end of last row, **do not** turn, fasten off.

Second Corner

Row 1: Working in ends of rows on Second Rectangle, join med. green with sc in row 5, (ch 1, skip next row, sc in next row) 2 times, sl st in row 1 on adjoining piece, turn (3 sc, 2 ch-1 sps).

Rows 2-5: Repeat same rows of Third Rectangle.

Third Corner

Row 1: Working in ends of rows on opposite edge of Second Rectangle, join med. green with sc in row 1, (ch 1, skip next row, sc in next row) 2 times, turn (3 sc, 2 ch-1 sps).

Rows 2-5: Repeat same rows of First Rectangle.

Fourth Rectangle

Row 1: Working across remaining side of Center Square, join dk. green with sc in first ch-2

Continued on page 77

Queen's Lace

Designer: Dot Drake

Size: 54½" x 86½" not including Tassels.

Materials: Size 10 bedspread acrylic thread; 2100 yds. each white and ecru; No. 7 steel crochet hook or size needed to obtain gauge.

Gauge: Rnds 1-3 of Motif = 2¼". Each Motif is 8¼" across.

Skill Level: ★★★★ Challenging

INSTRUCTIONS

FIRST ROW

First Motif

Rnd 1: With ecru, ch 5, sl st in first ch to form ring, ch 1, 12 sc in ring, join with sl st in first sc (12 sc).

Rnd 2: Ch 1, sc in first st, ch 7, skip next st, (sc in next st, ch 7, skip next st) around, join (6 ch-7 sps).

NOTES: For **beginning cluster (beg cl),** ch 4, *yo 2 times, insert hook in same sp, yo, draw lp through, (yo, draw through 2 lps on hook) 2 times; repeat from *, yo, draw through all 3 lps on hook.

For **cluster (cl),** *yo 2 times, insert hook in ch sp, yo, draw lp through, (yo, draw through 2 lps on hook) 2 times; repeat from * 2 more times in same sp, yo, draw through all 4 lps on hook.

Rnd 3: Sl st in each of next 2 chs, (beg cl, ch 7, sl st in 4th ch from hook, ch 3, cl) in same sp, ch 5, *(cl, ch 7, sl st in 4th ch from hook, ch 3, cl) in next ch sp, ch 5; repeat from * around, join with sl st in top of beg cl, fasten off (6 ch-5 sps).

Rnd 4: Join white with sl st in 3rd ch of any ch-5 sp, ch 13, *(dc, ch 3, dc) in 3rd ch of next ch-5 sp, ch 10; repeat from * around, dc in same ch as first sl st, ch 3, join with sl st in 3rd ch of ch-13 (6 ch-10 sps, 6 ch-3 sps).

Rnd 5: Sl st in first ch-10 sp, ch 4, 11 tr in same sp, ch 5, skip next ch-3 sp, (12 tr in next ch sp, ch 5, skip next ch-3 sp) around, join with sl st in top of ch-4 (72 tr, 6 ch-5 sps).

NOTES: For **picot,** ch 4, sl st in last sc made.

For **beginning decrease (beg dec),** ch 3, *yo 2 times, insert hook in next st, yo, draw lp through, (yo, draw through 2 lps on hook) 2 times; repeat from * 2 more times; yo, draw through all 4 lps on hook.

For **decrease (dec),** *yo 2 times, insert hook in next st, yo, draw lp through, (yo, draw through 2 lps on hook) 2 times; repeat from * 3 more times, yo, draw through all 5 lps on hook.

Rnd 6: Beg dec, *[ch 4, 2 tr in each of next 4 sts, ch 4, dec, ch 5, sc in next ch sp, picot], ch 5, dec; repeat from * 4 more times; repeat between [ ]; to **join,** ch 2, dc in beg dec. Joining (ch 2, dc) counts as a ch-5 sp.

NOTE: For **cluster (cl) on remaining rnds**, *yo 2 times, insert hook in next st, yo, draw lp through, (yo, draw through 2 lps on hook) 2 times, yo 2 times, insert hook in same st, yo, draw lp through, (yo, draw through 2 lps on hook) 2 times; repeat from *, yo, draw through all 5 lps on hook.

Rnd 7: Ch 11, *[skip next dec and next ch-4 sp, cl, ch 4, tr in next 4 sts, ch 4, cl, ch 7, skip next ch-4 sp, tr in next ch-5 sp], ch 2, tr in next ch-5 sp, ch 7; repeat from * 4 more times; repeat between [ ]; to **join,** ch 1, sc in 4th ch of ch-11.

Rnd 8: Ch 9, *[tr in next ch-7 sp, ch 9, skip next ch-4 sp, dec, ch 9, skip next ch-4 sp, tr in next ch-7 sp, ch 5], tr in next ch-2 sp, ch 5; repeat from * 4 more times; repeat between [ ], join with sl st in 4th ch of ch-9.

Rnd 9: Ch 1, sc in first st, *[6 sc in next ch-5 sp, sc in next st, (11 sc in next ch-9 sp, sc in next st) 2 times, 6 sc in next ch-5 sp], sc in next st; repeat from * 4 more times; repeat between [ ], join with sl st in first sc, fasten off (228 sc).

Rnd 10: Join ecru with sl st in st above any dec, ch 3, 2 dc in same st, dc in each st around with 3 dc in st above each dec, join with sl st in top of ch-3 (240 dc).

Rnd 11: Ch 5, dc in next st, ch 2, dc in next st, [*ch 1, skip next st, (dc in next st, ch 1, skip next st) 18 times], dc in next st, (ch 2, dc in next st) 2 times; repeat from * 4 more times; repeat between [ ], join with sl st in 3rd ch of ch-5, fasten off (126 dc, 114 ch-2 sps, 12 ch-2 sps).

Continued on page 68

Queen's Lace

continued from page 67

Rnd 12: Join white with sc in 2nd dc, picot, *[2 sc in next ch-2 sp, sc in next 5 sts and ch-1 sps, picot, (sc in next 6 sts and ch-1 sps, picot) 5 times, sc in next 4 sts and ch-1 sps, 2 sc in next ch-2 sp], sc in next st, picot; repeat from * 4 more times; repeat between [ ], join with sl st in first sc, fasten off (42 picots).

Second Motif

Rnds 1-11: Repeat same rnds of First Motif.

NOTE: For **joining picot,** ch 1, sc in corresponding picot on designated Motif, ch 1, sl st in top of last sc made on this Motif.

Rnd 12: Join white with sc in 2nd dc, picot, *[2 sc in next ch-2 sp, sc in next 5 sts and ch-1 sps, picot, (sc in next 6 sts and ch-1 sps, picot) 5 times, sc in next 4 sts and ch-1 sps, 2 sc in next ch-2 sp], sc in next st, picot; repeat from * 2 more times; repeat between [ ], sc in next st; joining to bottom edge of last Motif made (see Joining Diagram on page 69), work joining picot, 2 sc in next ch-2 sp, sc in next 5 sts and ch-1 sps, work joining picot, (sc in next 6 sts and ch-1 sps, work joining picot) 5 times, sc in next 4 sts and ch-1 sps, 2 sc in next ch-2 sp, sc in next st, work joining picot; repeat between [ ], join with sl st in first sc, fasten off.

Repeat Second Motif 8 more times for a total of 10 Motifs.

SECOND ROW

First Motif

Rnds 1-11: Repeat same rnds of First Motif on First Row.

Rnd 12: Join white with sc in 2nd dc, picot, *[2 sc in next ch-2 sp, sc in next 5 sts and ch-1 sps, picot, (sc in next 6 sts and ch-1 sps, picot) 5 times, sc in next 4 sts and ch-1 sps, 2 sc in next ch-2 sp], sc in next st, picot; repeat from *; repeat between [ ], sc in next st; joining to side of First Motif on last Row made (see Joining Diagram), work joining picot, ◊2 sc in next ch-2 sp, sc in next 5 sts and ch-1 sps, work joining picot, (sc in next 6 sts and ch-1 sps, work joining picot) 5 times, sc in next 4 sts and ch-1 sps, 2 sc in next ch-2 sp, sc in next st, work joining picot◊; joining to side of next Motif on last Row made; repeat between ◊◊; repeat between [ ], join with sl st in first sc, fasten off.

Second Motif

Rnds 1-11: Repeat same rnds of First Motif on First Row.

Rnd 12: Join white with sc in 2nd dc, picot, *2 sc in next ch-2 sp, sc in next 5 sts and ch-1 sps, picot, (sc in next 6 sts and ch-1 sps, picot) 5 times, sc in next 4 sts and ch-1 sps, 2 sc in next ch-2 sp*, sc in next st, picot; repeat between **, sc in next st; joining to bottom of last Motif on this Row (see Joining Diagram), work joining picot, [2 sc in next ch-2 sp, sc in next 5 sts and ch-1 sps, work joining picot, (sc in next 6 sts and ch-1 sps, work joining picot) 5 times, sc in next 4 sts and ch-1 sps, 2 sc in next ch-2 sp, sc in next st, work joining picot]; joining to side of corresponding Motif on last Row made; repeat between [ ]; joining to side of next Motif on last Row made; repeat between [ ]; repeat between **, join with sl st in first sc, fasten off.

Repeat Second Motif 7 more times for a total of 9 Motifs.

THIRD ROW

First Motif

Rnds 1-11: Repeat same rnds of First Motif on First Row.

Rnd 12: Joining to side of First Motif on last Row made (see Joining Diagram), work same as Second Motif on First Row.

Repeat Second Motif on Second Row 9 more times for a total of 10 Motifs.

Repeat Second and Third Row alternately, for a total of 7 Rows.

TASSEL (make 36)

For **each Tassel,** cut 50 strands ecru each 10" long. Tie separate strand tightly around middle of all strands; fold strands in half. Wrap separate 6" strand 1" from top of fold; secure. Trim ends.

Starting at bottom of fold, with ecru, insert hook through center of fold, yo, draw lp through, yo, draw through 2 lps on hook (sc made), work 40 more sc around fold, join with sl st in first sc, fasten off.

BORDER

NOTES: For **treble decrease (tr dec),** *yo 2 times, insert hook in next picot, yo, draw lp through, (yo, draw through 2 lps on hook) 2 times*, skip next joined picots; repeat between **, yo, draw through all 3 lps on hook.

For **double treble decrease (dtr dec),** *yo 3 times, insert hook in next picot, yo, draw lp through, (yo, draw through 2 lps on hook) 3 times*, skip next joined picots; repeat between **, yo, draw through all 3 lps on hook.

For **beginning shell (beg shell),** ch 6, dc in same picot, (ch 3, dc in same picot) 2 times.

For **shell,** dc in next picot, (ch 3, dc in same picot) 3 times.

Rnd 1: Working around outer edge, join white with sl st in indicated unworked picot of First Motif

on First Row (see Joining Diagram), beg shell, [*ch 5, (dc in next picot, ch 5) 5 times, tr dec, ch 5, (dc in next picot, ch 5) 5 times, shell; repeat from * 8 more times, ch 5, (dc in next picot, ch 5) 6 times, shell, ch 5, (dc in next picot, ch 5) 6 times, shell, ◊ch 5, (dc in next picot, ch 5) 5 times, dtr dec, ch 5, (dc in next picot, ch 5) 4 times, dtr dec, ch 5, (dc in next picot, ch 5) 5 times, shell, ch 5, (dc in next picot, ch 5) 6 times, shell; repeat from ◊ 2 more times, ch 5, (dc in next picot, ch 5) 6 times], shell; repeat between [ ], join with sl st in 3rd ch of ch-6.

Rnd 2: Sl st in first ch-3 sp, ch 1, 4 sc in same sp, 4 sc in each ch-3 sp, 8 sc in each ch-5 sp and 4 sc in ch-5 sps on each side of decs, join with sl st in first sc.

Rnd 3: Beg dec, (ch 5, dec) 2 times, ch 7, skip next 2 sts, dec, (ch 7, skip next 4 sts, dec) across to 2 sts before 12 sts over next shell, ch 7, skip next 2 sts, *dec, (ch 5, dec) 2 times, ch 7, skip next 2 sts, dec, (ch 7, skip next 4 sts, dec) across to 2 sts before 12 sts over next shell, ch 7, skip next 2 sts; repeat from * around, join with sl st in top of beg dec.

NOTE: For **double crochet decrease (dc dec),** (yo, insert hook in next ch sp, yo, draw lp through, yo, draw through 2 lps on hook) 2 times, yo, draw through all 3 lps on hook.

Rnd 4: Sl st in first ch sp, ch 1, sc in same sp, ch 7, (sc in next ch sp, ch 7) around with (dc dec, ch 7) at each indentation, join with sl st in frst sc, fasten off.

NOTE: For **scallop,** (ch 3, sl st, ch 5, sl st, ch 3, sl st) in top of last sc made.

Rnd 5: Join ecru with sc in 2nd ch sp, 4 sc in same sp, scallop, 5 sc in same ch sp, *5 sc in next ch sp, scallop, 5 sc in same ch sp) across to one ch sp before next dec, 5 sc in next ch sp, scallop, 5 sc in next ch sp; repeat between ( ) across to ch sp at next point, 5 sc in next ch sp; to **join Tassel,** ch 1, sc in center sc on top of any Tassel, ch 1; 5 sc in same sp on this rnd; repeat from * around, join, fasten off.✣

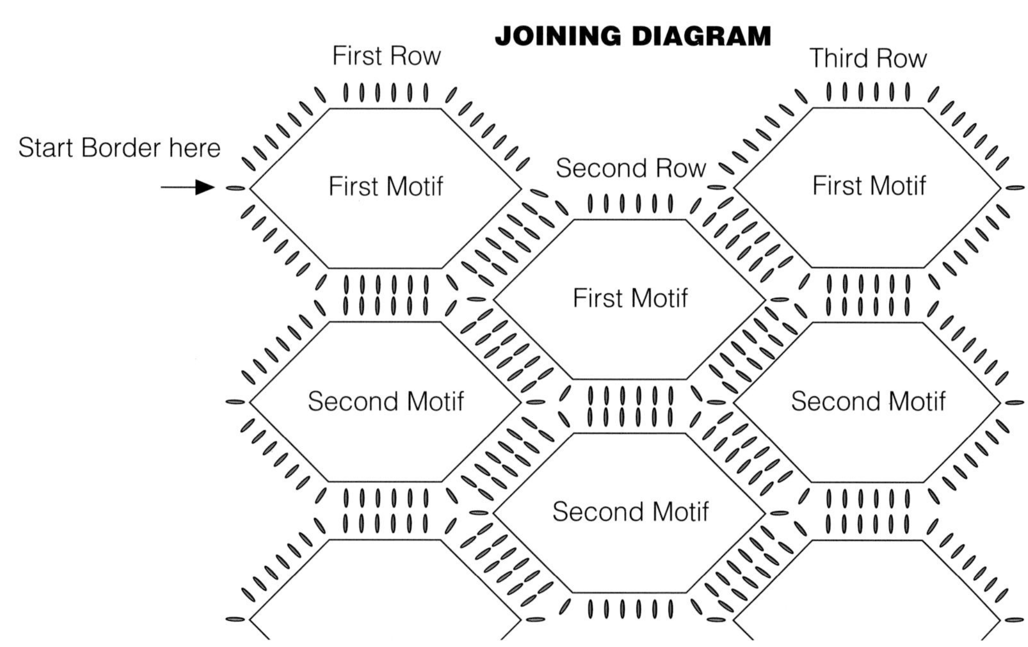

Regal Tapestry

Designer: Dot Drake

Size: 60" x 78"

Materials: Worsted-weight yarn — 16 oz. each, rose, dk. teal, burgundy, spruce, 12 oz. off-white; H crochet hook or size needed to obtain gauge.

Gauge: 7 sc = 2"; 2 dc rows and 1 sc row = 2"".

Skill Level: ★★ Average

INSTRUCTIONS

AFGHAN

NOTES: For **front post st (fp)**, yo, insert hook from front to back around post of st on last row, yo, draw lp through, complete as dc.

Row 1: With off-white, ch 273, sc in 2nd ch from hook, sc in each ch across, turn (272 sc).

Row 2: Ch 1, sc in each st across, fasten off, turn.

Row 3: Join rose with sl st in first st, ch 3, dc in each st across, turn.

Row 4: Ch 4, (skip next st, dc in each of next 2 sts; working in front of sts, fp around skipped st, ch 1) across to last st, dc in last st, turn.

Row 5: Ch 3, (dc in each of next 2 dc, tr around post st) across to ch-4, dc in 3rd ch of ch-4, turn.

Row 6: Ch 1, sc in each st across, fasten off.

Row 7: Join off-white with sc in first st, sc in each st across, turn.

Rows 8-128: Following color sequence of dk. teal, burgundy, spruce and rose, repeat rows 2-7 consecutively ending with row 2. At end of last row, **do not** turn or fasten off.

BORDER

Row 1: Working in ends of rows, 2 sc in each dc row and sc in each sc row across, turn.

Row 2: Ch 1, sc in each st across, fasten off.

Row 3: Working in ends of rows on oppostie side, with right side facing you, join with sc in end of first row, sc in each sc row and 2 dc in each dc row, across, turn.

Row 4: Ch 1, sc in each st across, turn.

Rnd 5: Working around entire outer edge, sl st in each st around, join with sl st in first sl st, fasten off.✣

Roses at Midnight

Designer: Katherine Eng

Size: 40" x 60".

Materials: Fuzzy worsted-weight yarn — 36 oz. coral/blue/plum variegated and 14 oz. coral; tapestry needle; H crochet hook or size needed to obtain gauge.

Gauge: Rnds 1-2 of Block = 2¾" across. Block is 6¾" across.

Skill Level: ★★ Average

INSTRUCTIONS

BLOCK (make 40)

Rnd 1: With variegated, ch 4, sl st in first ch to form ring, ch 3, 2 dc in ring, ch 2, (3 dc in ring, ch 2) 3 times, join with sl st in top of ch-3 (12 dc, 4 ch-2 sps).

Rnd 2: Sl st in next st, ch 1, sc in same st, *[ch 1, skip next st, (sc, ch 2, sc) in next ch sp, ch 1, skip next st], sc in next st; repeat from * 2 more times; repeat between [ ], join with sl st in first sc (12 sc, 8 ch-1 sps, 4 ch-2 sps).

Rnd 3: Ch 1, sc in each st and in each ch-1 sp around with (sc, ch 2, sc) in each corner ch-2 sp, join, **turn** (28 sc, 4 ch-2 sps).

Rnd 4: Ch 1, sc in each st around with (sc, ch 2, sc) in each corner ch-2 sp, join, **turn** (36 sc, 4 ch-2 sps).

Rnd 5: Ch 4, skip next st, (dc in next st, ch 1, skip next st) 2 times, *(2 dc, ch 2, 2 dc) in next ch sp, ch 1, skip next st, (dc in next st, ch 1, skip next st) across to next corner; repeat from * 2 more times; (2 dc, ch 2, 2 dc) in next ch sp, ch 1, skip next st, dc in next st, ch 1, skip last st, join with sl st in 3rd ch of ch-4, **turn**.

Rnd 6: Repeat rnd 3, fasten off (60 sc, 4 ch-2 sps).

Rnd 7: Join coral with sc in any corner ch-2 sp, ch 2, sc in same sp, *[ch 1, skip next st, (sc in next st, ch 1, skip next st) across] to next corner ch-2 sp, (sc, ch 2, sc) in next ch-2 sp; repeat from * 2 more times; repeat between [ ], join, fasten off (36 sc, 32 ch-1 sps, 4 ch-2 sps).

Rnd 8: Join variegated with sc in any corner ch-2 sp, ch 2, sc in same sp, *[ch 1, (sc in next ch-1 sp, ch 1) across] to next corner ch-2 sp, (sc, ch 2, sc) in next ch-2 sp; repeat from * 2 more times; repeat between [ ], join, fasten off (40 sc, 36 ch-1 sps, 4 ch-2 sps).

Flower

Rnd 1: Leaving 6" end for sewing, with coral, ch 4, sl st in first ch to form ring, ch 1, (sc, ch 3) 6 times in ring, join with sl st in first sc (6 sc, 6 ch-3 sps).

Rnd 2: Ch 1; working behind rnd 1, sc in sp between first 2 sc, ch 5, (sc in sp between next 2 sc, ch 5) around, join, fasten off.

Sew to center of Block.

ASSEMBLY

Holding Blocks wrong sides together, matching sts, with variegated, sew together through **back lps,** in 5 rows of 8 Blocks each.

BORDER

Rnd 1: Working around outer edge, join variegated with sc in any corner ch-2 sp, ch 3, sc in same sp, sc in each st, sc in each ch-1 sp, sc in ch sps on each side of seams and hdc in each seam around with (sc, ch 3, sc) in each corner ch-2 sp, join with sl st in first sc, **turn.**

Rnd 2: Sl st in next st, ch 1, sc in same st, *ch 1, skip next st, (sc in next st, ch 1, skip next st) across to next corner ch-3 sp, (sc, ch 3, sc) in next ch-3 sp; repeat from * 3 more times, ch 1, skip last st, join, **turn,** fasten off.

Rnd 3: Join coral with sl st in any corner ch-3 sp, ch 3, (dc, ch 2, 2 dc) in same sp, dc in each st and in each ch-1 sp around with (2 dc, ch 2, 2 dc) in each corner ch-3 sp, join with sl st in top of ch-3, **turn,** fasten off.

Rnd 4: Join variegated with sl st in any corner ch-2 sp, ch 4, (dc, ch 2, dc, ch 1, dc) in same sp, *[ch 1, skip next st, (dc in next st, ch 1, skip next st) across] to next corner ch-2 sp, (dc, ch 1, dc, ch 2, dc, ch 1, dc) in next ch-2 sp; repeat from * 2

Continued on page 76

Royal Satin

Designer: Dorris Brooks

Size: 43" x 64" not including Fringe.

Materials: Worsted-weight yarn — 38½ oz. dk. pink; J crochet hook or size needed to obtain gauge.

Gauge: 1 dc shell = 1½"; 4 rows = 3".

Skill Level: ★ Easy

INSTRUCTIONS

AFGHAN

NOTES: For **cluster (cl),** yo, insert hook in next st or ch sp, yo, draw lp through, yo, draw through 2 lps on hook, (yo, insert hook in same st or ch sp, yo, draw lp through, yo, draw through 2 lps on hook) 2 times, yo, draw through all 4 lps on hook.

For **shell,** 5 dc in next st.

Row 1: Ch 125, sc in 2nd ch from hook, sc in each ch across, turn (124 sc).

Row 2: Ch 3, skip next st, (cl, ch 1, cl) in next st, *skip next 3 sts, shell in next st, skip next 3 sts, (cl, ch 1, cl) in next st; repeat from * across to last st, dc in last st, turn (32 cls, 16 ch-1 sps, 15 shells).

Rows 3-84: Ch 3, skip next st, (cl, ch 1, cl) in next ch-1 sp, *shell in center st of next shell, (cl, ch 1, cl) in next ch-1 sp; repeat from * across to last st, dc in last st, turn.

Row 85: Ch 1, sc in each st or ch sp across, **do not** turn or fasten off.

EDGING

Working in end rows, shell in first row, (sc in next row, shell in next row) across, fasten off.

Working on opposite edge, join with sl st in end of first row, ch 3, 4 dc in same row, (sc in next row, shell in next row) across, fasten off.

FRINGE

For **each Fringe,** cut 3 strands each 16" long. With all three strands held together, fold in half, insert hook in st, draw fold through, draw all loose ends through fold, tighten. Trim ends.

Fringe in every other st on each short end of Afghan.✣

Crystal Treasure

continued from page 63

st in first st, sl st in next ch sp, ch 1, sc in same sp, (V-st in next sc, sc in next V-st) across, turn.

Rows 6-7: Repeat rows 4 and 5.

Row 8: Working this row in **back lps** only, ch 1, sl st in each st and in each ch across, turn, fasten off.

Row 9: Working in **remaining lps** of row 7, join med. pink with sc in first st, (ch 1, skip next st or ch, sc in next st or ch) across, **do not** turn, fasten off (105 sc, 104 ch-1 sps).

NOTE: For **long single crochet (lsc),** working over next ch sp, sc in next skipped st or ch on row before last.

Row 10: Join white with sc in first st, lsc, (ch 1, skip next st, lsc) across to last st, sc in last st, **do not** turn, fasten off (104 lsc, 103 ch-1 sps, 2 sc).

Row 11: Join med. pink with sc in first st, ch 1, skip next st, (lsc, ch 1, skip next st) across to last st, sc in last st, **do not** turn, fasten off (104 ch-1 sps, 103 lsc, 2 sc).

Row 12: Join white with sc in first st, (2 lsc in next lsc on row before last) across to last lsc, lsc in last lsc, sc same lsc and last st on last row tog, fasten off (209 sc).

Repeat on opposite edge.

With H hook and white, hold 2 Strips right sides together; matching sts of last row on Border, sc Strips together. Repeat with remaining Strips.

EDGING

Working in sts and in ends of rows across one short end, with H hook and white, join with sc in first row, sc evenly across to opposite corner, fasten off.

Repeat on opposite end.

FRINGE

For **each Fringe,** cut one strand white 16" long. Fold in half, insert hook in st, draw fold through, draw all loose ends through fold, tighten, trim ends.

Fringe in each st across short ends of Afghan.✣

Roses at Midnight

continued from page 73

more times; repeat between [ ], join with sl st in 3rd ch of ch-4, **turn,** fasten off.

Rnd 5: Join coral with sl st in any corner ch-2 sp, ch 3, (dc, ch 2, 2 dc) in same sp, dc in each st and in each ch-1 sp around with (2 dc, ch 2, 2 dc) in each corner ch-2 sp, join, **turn.**

Rnd 6: Ch 1, sc in first st, *ch 1, skip next st, (sc in next st, ch 1, skip next st) across to next corner ch-2 sp, (sc, ch 3, sc) in next ch-2 sp; repeat from * 3 more times, ch 1, skip last st, join with sl st in first sc, **turn,** fasten off.

Rnd 7: Join variegated with sc in any corner ch-3 sp, ch 3, sc in same sp, sc in each st and in each ch-1 sp around with (sc, ch 3, sc) in each corner ch-3 sp, join, **do not** turn.

Rnd 8: Sl st in next ch-3 sp, ch 1, (sc, ch 3, sc, ch 4, sc, ch 3, sc) in same sp, ◊[skip next st, *(sc, ch 3, sc) in next st, skip next st; repeat from * across] to next corner ch-3 sp, (sc, ch 3, sc, ch 4, sc, ch 3, sc) in next ch-3 sp; repeat from ◊ 2 more times; repeat between [ ], join, fasten off.✣

Imperial Jade

continued from page 64

sp, ch 1, skip next st, (sc in next st, ch 1, skip next st) 5 times, sc in next ch-2 sp, sl st in row 1 of adjoining piece, turn (7 sc, 6 ch-1 sps).

Rows 2-5: Repeat same rows of Third Rectangle.

Fourth Corner

Row 1: Working in ends of rows across opposite edge of First Rectangle, join med. green with sc in row 5, (ch 1, skip next row, sc in next row) 2 times, sl st in row 1 of adjoining piece (3 sc, 2 ch-1 sps).

Rows 2-5: Repeat same rows of Third Rectangle.

Edging

Working in sts and in ends of rows around outer edge, join dk. pink with sc in any corner, ch 2, sc in same corner, *[ch 1, skip next row or ch-1 sp, (sc in next row, ch-1 sp or joining sl st, ch 1, skip next row, ch-1 sp or joining sl st) across] to next corner, (sc, ch 3, sc) in next corner; repeat from * 2 more times; repeat between [ ], join with sl st in first sc, fasten off (13 sc and 12 ch-1 sps between each corner ch-3 sp).

Holding Blocks wrong sides together, matching sts and chs, with dk. pink, sew together through **back lps**, in five rows of eight Blocks each.

BORDER

Rnd 1: Working around outer edge, join dk. pink with sc in any corner ch-3 sp, ch 3, sc in same sp, sc in each st, in each ch-1 sp, in ch-3 sps on each side of seams and hdc in each seam around with (sc, ch 3, sc) in each corner ch-3 sp, join with sl st in first sc, **turn** (139 dc on each short end between corner ch-3 sps, 223 sc on each long edge between corner ch-3 sps).

Rnd 2: Sl st in next st, ch 1, sc in same st, *ch 1, skip next st, (sc in next st, ch 1, skip next st) across to next corner ch-3 sp, (sc, ch 3, sc) in next ch-3 sp; repeat from * 3 more times, ch 1, skip last st, join, **turn,** fasten off.

Rnd 3: Join med. green with sc in any corner ch-3 sp, ch 3, sc in same sp, *[sc in next st, (ch 1, skip next ch-1 sp, sc in next st) across] to next corner ch-3 sp, (sc, ch 3, sc) in next ch-3 sp; repeat from * 2 more times; repeat between [ ], join, **do not** turn.

Rnd 4: Ch 3, dc in each st and in each ch-1 sp around with (2 dc, ch 3, 2 dc) in each corner ch-3 sp, join with sl st in top of ch-3, **turn**.

Rnd 5: Sl st in next st, ch 1, sc in same st, *ch 1, skip next st, (sc in next st, ch 1, skip next st) across to next corner ch-3 sp, (sc, ch 3, sc) in next ch-3 sp; repeat from * 3 more times, ch 1, skip next st, sc in next st, ch 1, skip last st, join with sl st in first sc, **turn.**

Rnd 6: Repeat rnd 4, **do not** turn, fasten off (153 dc on each short end between corner ch-3 sps, 237 dc on each long edge between corner ch-3 sps).

Rnd 7: Join dk. green with sl st in any corner ch-3 sp, (ch 3, 2 dc, ch 3, 3 dc) in same sp, [◊skip next st, sc in next st, *skip next 2 sts, (2 dc, ch 2, 2 dc) in next st, skip next 2 sts, sc in next st; repeat from * across to one st before next corner ch sp, skip next st◊, (3 dc, ch 3, 3 dc) in next corner ch sp; repeat between [ ] 2 more times; repeat between ◊◊, join.

Rnd 8: Sl st in next st, ch 1, (sc, ch 3, sc) in same st, ◊[ch 1, skip next st, (sc, ch 3, sc, ch 5, sc, ch 3, sc) in next corner ch-3 sp, ch 1, skip next st, (sc, ch 3, sc) in next st, ch 1, skip next st, sc in next sc, *ch 2, (sc, ch 3, sc) in next ch-2 sp, ch 2, sc in next sc; repeat from * across to 3 dc before next corner ch-3 sp, ch 1, skip next st], (sc, ch 3, sc) in next st; repeat from ◊ 2 more times; repeat between [ ], join with sl st in first sc, fasten off.✣

ASSEMBLY DIAGRAM

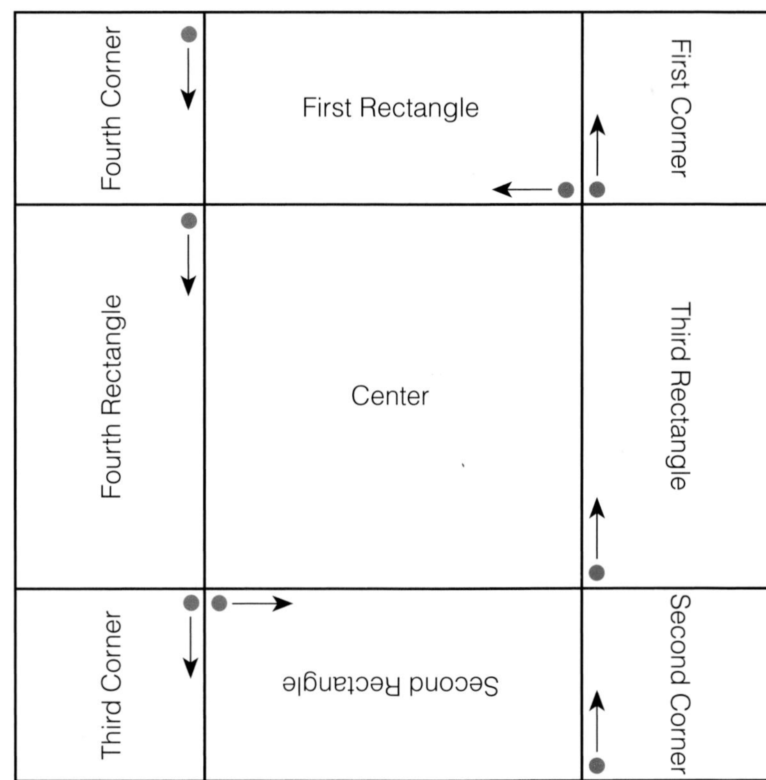

Little One's Path

"One walked between his wife and child,
With measured footfall firm and mild, …
… The little maiden walked demure,
Pacing with downward eyelids pure. …"

—LORD ALFRED TENNYSON

Tender Touch

Designer: Katherine Eng

Size: 33" x 40".

Materials: Worsted-weight yarn — 10 oz. pastel variegated and 7 oz. pink; I crochet hook or size needed to obtain gauge.

Gauge: 6 sc and 5 ch-1 sps = 3"; 3 sc rows worked in front lps only = 1".

Skill Level: ★★ Average

INSTRUCTIONS

AFGHAN

Row 1: With pastel variegated, ch 130, sc in 2nd ch from hook, (ch 1, skip next ch, sc in next ch) across, turn (65 sc, 64 ch-1 sps).

Rows 2-6: Working these rows in **front lps** only, ch 1, sc in first st, (ch 1, skip next ch sp, sc in next st) across, turn. At end of last row, fasten off.

Row 7: Working in **both lps,** join pink with sc in first st, (ch 3, skip next ch sp, skip next st, skip next ch sp, sc in next st) across, turn.

Row 8: Ch 1, sc in first st, (ch 3, skip next ch-3 sp, sc in next st) across, turn, fasten off.

Row 9: Join pastel variegated with sc in first st, (ch 1, sc in next ch-3 sp, ch 1, sc in next st) across, turn.

Rows 10-12: Repeat row 2. At end of last row, fasten off.

Rows 13-15: Repeat rows 7-9.

Rows 16-76: Repeat rows 2-15 consecutively, ending with row 6.

BORDER

Rnd 1: Working around outer edge, with right side facing you, join pink with sc in first st on last row, ch 2, sc in same st, *sc in next ch-1 sp, (ch 1, skip next st, sc in next ch-1 sp) across to last st, (sc, ch 2, sc) in last st; working in ends of rows, ch 1, skip next row, (sc in next row, ch 1, skip next row) across*; working in starting ch on opposite side of row 1, (sc, ch 2, sc) in first ch; repeat between **, join with sl st in first sc (66 sc and 63 ch-1 sps across each long edge between corner ch-2 sps, 39 sc and 38 ch-1 sps across each short end between corner ch-2 sps).

Rnd 2: Ch 1, sc in first st, (sc, ch 2, sc) in next ch-2 sp, sc in each st and in each ch-1 sp around with (sc, ch 2, sc) in each corner ch-2 sp, join (131 sc across each long edge between corner ch-2 sps, 79 sc across each short end between corner ch-2 sps).

Rnd 3: Sl st in next st, sl st in next ch-2 sp, ch 1, (sc, ch 3, sc) in same sp, *[ch 3, skip next 3 sts, (sc in next st, ch 3, skip next 3 sts) across to next corner ch-2 sp], (sc, ch 3, sc) in next ch-2 sp; repeat from * 2 more times; repeat between [ ], join.

NOTES: For **shell,** (hdc, dc, ch 2, dc, hdc) in next ch sp

For **corner shell,** (2 dc, ch 2, 2 dc) in next ch sp.

Rnd 4: Ch 1, sc in first st, *[corner shell in next corner ch-3 sp, (sc in next st, shell in next ch-3 sp) across] to last st before next corner ch-3 sp, sc in next st; repeat from * 2 more times; repeat between [ ], join, **turn,** fasten off.

Rnd 5: Join pastel variegated with sc in ch sp of any corner shell, ch 1, (sc, ch 3, sc) in same sp, ◊[ch 2, sc in next sc between shells, ch 2, *(sc, ch 2, sc) in ch sp of next shell, ch 2, sc in next sc between shells, ch 2; repeat from * across to next corner shell], (sc, ch 3, sc) in ch sp of next corner shell; repeat from ◊ 2 more times; repeat between [ ], join, **turn,** fasten off.

Rnd 6: Join pink with sc in any corner ch-3 sp, (ch 3, sc, ch 4, sc, ch 3, sc) in same sp, ◊[(sc, ch 3, sc) in next ch-2 sp, sc in next ch-2 sp, (sc, ch 2, sc) in next ch-2 sp, *sc in each of next 2 ch-2 sps, (sc, ch 3, sc) in next ch-2 sp; repeat from * across to last 2 ch-2 sps before next corner ch-3 sp, sc in next ch-2 sp, (sc, ch 3, sc) in next ch-2 sp], (sc, ch 3, sc, ch 4, sc, ch 3, sc) in next corner ch-3 sp; repeat from ◊ 2 more times; repeat between [ ], join, fasten off.✣

Dainty Delight

Designer: Darla J. Fanton

Size: 38" x 41".

Materials: Worsted-weight yarn — 21 oz. white; G crochet hook or size needed to obtain gauge.

Gauge: 4 dc = 1"; 7 dc rows = 3".

Skill Level: ★★ Average

INSTRUCTIONS

AFGHAN

NOTE: Back of row 1 is right side of work.

Row 1: Ch 145, dc in 4th ch from hook, dc in each ch across, turn (143 dc).

Row 2: Ch 3, dc in next 10 sts, (ch 1, skip next st, dc in next 11 sts) across, turn (132 dc, 11 ch-1 sps).

Row 3: Ch 4, skip next st, dc in next 7 sts, *ch 1, skip next st, (dc in next st, ch 1, skip next st) 2 times, dc in next 7 sts; repeat from * across to last 2 sts, ch 1, skip next st, dc in last st, turn (108 dc, 35 ch-1 sps).

Row 4: Ch 4, skip next ch-1 sp, *[dc in next st, ch 1, skip next st, dc in each of next 3 sts, ch 1, skip next st, dc in next st, ch 1, skip next ch-1 sp], dc in next st, dc in next ch-1 sp, dc in next st, ch 1, skip next ch-1 sp; repeat from * 10 more times; repeat between [ ], dc in 3rd ch of last ch-4, turn (95 dc, 48 ch-1 sps).

Row 5: Ch 3, dc in next ch-1 sp, dc in next st, *[ch 1, skip next ch-1 sp, (dc in next st, ch 1, skip next st or ch-1 sp) 2 times, dc in next st, dc in next ch-1 sp], dc in each of next 3 sts, dc in next ch-1 sp, dc in next st; repeat from * 10 more times; repeat between [ ], dc in 3rd ch of last ch-4, turn (107 dc, 36 ch-1 sps).

Row 6: Ch 3, dc in each of next 2 sts, dc in next ch-1 sp, dc in next st, *[ch 1, skip next ch-1 sp, dc in next st, dc in next ch-1 sp], dc in next 7 sts, dc in next ch-1 sp, dc in next st; repeat from * 10 more times; repeat between [ ], dc in each of last 3 sts, turn (131 dc, 12 ch-1 sps).

Row 7: Ch 3, dc in next 4 sts, *dc in next ch-1 sp, dc in next 5 sts, ch 1, skip next st, dc in next 5 sts; repeat from * 10 more times, dc in next ch-1 sp, dc in last 5 sts, turn (132 dc, 11 ch-1 sps).

Rows 8-91: Repeat rows 3-7 consecutively, ending with row 6.

Row 92: Ch 3, dc in each st and in each ch-1 sp across, **do not** turn, fasten off (143 dc).

BORDER

Rnd 1: Working around outer edge, with right side facing you, join with sc in first st on last row, ch 3, sc in same st, sc in each st and 2 sc in end of each row around with (sc, ch 3, sc) in each corner, join with sl st in first sc (143 sc across each short end between corner ch-3 sps, 186 sc across each long edge between corner ch-3 sps).

Rnd 2: Sl st in first corner ch-3 sp, ch 1, (sc, ch 3, sc) in same sp, *ch 2, skip next 2 sts, (sc in next st, ch 2, skip next 2 sts) across to next corner ch-3 sp, (sc, ch 3, sc) in next ch-3 sp, ch 2, skip next st, (sc in next st, ch 2, skip next 2 sts) across to last 2 sts before next corner ch-3 sp, sc in next st, ch 2, skip next st*, (sc, ch 3, sc) in next corner ch-3 sp; repeat between **, join.

NOTE: For **beginning shell (beg shell),** ch 3, (2 dc, ch 3, 3 dc) in same ch sp.

For **shell,** (3 dc, ch 3, 3 dc) in next ch sp.

Rnd 3: Sl st in first corner ch-3 sp, beg shell, *[sc in next ch-2 sp, (shell in next ch-2 sp, sc in next ch-2 sp) across] to next corner ch-3 sp, shell in next ch-3 sp; repeat from * 2 more times; repeat between [ ], join with sl st in top of ch-3, fasten off.✣

Gentle Hearts

Designer: Erma Fielder

Size: 32" x 42".

Materials: Pompadour baby yarn — 30 oz. pink; H crochet hook or size needed to obtain gauge.

Gauge: 7 dc = 2"; 4 post sts worked in pattern = 1". 4 dc rows and 3 hdc rows = 3".

Skill Level: ★★★★ Challenging

INSTRUCTIONS

AFGHAN

Row 1: Ch 133, sc in 2nd ch from hook, sc in each ch across, turn (132 sc).

Row 2: Ch 3, dc in each st across, turn.

NOTES: For **double crochet back post (dc bp),** yo, insert hook from back to front around post of next st, yo, draw lp through, (yo, draw through 2 lps on hook) 2 times.

For **treble crochet front post (tr fp),** yo 2 times, insert hook from front to back around post of next st, yo, draw lp through, (yo, draw through 2 lps on hook) 3 times.

For **popcorn (pc),** 4 dc in next st, drop lp from hook, insert hook in first st of 4-dc group, draw dropped lp through, ch 1.

For **double crochet front post (dc fp),** yo, insert hook from front to back around post of next st, yo, draw lp through, (yo, draw through 2 lps on hook) 2 times.

Row 3: Ch 3, [*dc bp around each of next 2 sts, skip next st, tr fp around next st; working in front of fp just made, tr fp around skipped st, dc bp around each of next 2 sts*, dc in next 8 sts, pc, dc in next 8 sts; repeat between **], for **Pattern Repeat A,** (skip next 2 sts, tr fp around each of next 2 sts; working behind sts just made, dc in each of 2 skipped sts, skip next 2 sts, dc in each of next 2 sts; working in front of sts just made, tr fp around 2 skipped sts) 9 times; repeat between [ ], dc in last st, turn (70 dc, 44 tr fp, 16 dc bp, 2 pc).

Row 4: Ch 3, [*dc fp around each of next 2 sts, dc bp around each of next 2 sts, dc fp around each of next 2 sts*, hdc in next 17 sts; repeat between **], dc bp around each of next 2 sts, dc in next 4 sts, (dc bp around next 4 sts, dc in next 4 sts) 8 times, dc bp around each of next 2 sts; repeat between [ ], dc in last st, turn (44 dc bp, 38 dc, 34 hdc, 16 dc fp).

Row 5: Ch 3, [*dc bp around each of next 2 sts, skip next st, tr fp around next st; working in front of fp just made, tr fp around skipped st, dc bp around each of next 2 sts*, dc in next 5 sts, (pc, dc in next 5 sts) 2 times; repeat between **], for **Pattern Repeat B,** (skip next 2 sts, dc in each of next 2 sts; working in front of sts just made, tr fp around each of 2 skipped sts, skip next 2 sts, tr fp around each of next 2 sts; working behind sts just made, dc in each of 2 skipped sts) 9 times; repeat between [ ], dc in last st, turn.

Row 6: Ch 3, [*dc fp around each of next 2 sts, dc bp around each of next 2 sts, dc fp around each of next 2 sts*, hdc in next 17 sts; repeat between **], dc in each of next 2 sts, dc bp around next 4 sts, (dc in next 4 sts, dc bp around next 4 sts) 8 times, dc in each of next 2 sts; repeat between [ ], dc in last st, turn.

Row 7: Ch 3, [*dc bp around each of next 2 sts, skip next st, tr fp around next st; working in front of fp just made, tr fp around skipped st, dc bp around each of next 2 sts*, dc in each of next 3 sts, pc, dc in next 9 sts, pc, dc in each of next 3 sts; repeat between **], for **Pattern Repeat A,** (skip next 2 sts, tr fp around each of next 2 sts; working behind sts just made, dc in each of 2 skipped sts, skip next 2 sts, dc in each of next 2 sts; working in front of sts just made, tr fp around 2 skipped sts) 9 times; repeat between [ ], dc in last st, turn.

Row 8: Repeat row 4.

Row 9: Ch 3, [*dc bp around each of next 2 sts, skip next st, tr fp around next st; working in front of fp just made, tr fp around skipped st, dc bp around each of next 2 sts*, dc in next st, pc, dc in next 13 sts, pc, dc in next st; repeat between **], for **Pattern Repeat B,** (skip next 2 sts, dc in each of next 2 sts; working in front of sts just made, tr fp around each of 2 skipped sts, skip

Continued on page 86

THE TALE OF
The Flopsy Bunnies

Gentle Hearts

continued from page 84

next 2 sts, tr fp around each of next 2 sts; working behind sts just made, dc in each of 2 skipped sts) 9 times; repeat between [ ], dc in last st, turn.

Row 10: Repeat row 6.

Row 11: Ch 3, [*dc bp around each of next 2 sts, skip next st, tr fp around next st; working in front of fp just made, tr fp around skipped st, dc bp around each of next 2 sts*, dc in each of next 2 sts, pc, (dc in next 5 sts, pc) 2 times, dc in each of next 2 sts; repeat between **], for **Pattern Repeat A,** (skip next 2 sts, tr fp around each of next 2 sts; working behind sts just made, dc in each of 2 skipped sts, skip next 2 sts, dc in each of next 2 sts; working in front of sts just made, tr fp around 2 skipped sts) 9 times; repeat between [ ], dc in last st, turn.

Rows 12-14: Repeat rows 4-6.

Row 15: Ch 3, [*dc bp around each of next 2 sts, skip next st, tr fp around next st; working in front of fp just made, tr fp around skipped st, dc bp around each of next 2 sts*, dc in next 17 sts; repeat between **], for **Pattern Repeat A,** (skip next 2 sts, tr fp around each of next 2 sts; working behind sts just made, dc in each of 2 skipped sts, skip next 2 sts, dc in each of next 2 sts; working in front of sts just made, tr fp around 2 skipped sts) 9 times; repeat between [ ], dc in last st, turn.

Row 16: Repeat row 4.

Row 17: Ch 3, [*dc bp around each of next 2 sts, skip next st, tr fp around next st; working in front of fp just made, tr fp around skipped st, dc bp around each of next 2 sts*, dc in next 8 sts, pc, dc in next 8 sts; repeat between **], for **Pattern Repeat B,** (skip next 2 sts, dc in each of next 2 sts; working in front of sts just made, tr fp around each of 2 skipped sts, skip next 2 sts, tr fp around each of next 2 sts; working behind sts just made, dc in each of 2 skipped sts) 9 times; repeat between [ ], dc in last st, turn.

Row 18: Repeat row 6.

Row 19: Ch 3, [*dc bp around each of next 2 sts, skip next st, tr fp around next st; working in front of fp just made, tr fp around skipped st, dc bp around each of next 2 sts*, dc in next 5 sts, (pc, dc in next 5 sts) 2 times; repeat between **], for **Pattern Repeat A,** (skip next 2 sts, tr fp around each of next 2 sts; working behind sts just made, dc in each of 2 skipped sts, skip next 2 sts, dc in each of next 2 sts; working in front of sts just made, tr fp around 2 skipped sts) 9 times; repeat between [ ], dc in last st, turn.

Row 20: Repeat row 4.

Row 21: Ch 3, [*dc bp around each of next 2 sts, skip next st, tr fp around next st; working in front of fp just made, tr fp around skipped st, dc bp around each of next 2 sts*, dc in each of next 3 sts, pc, dc in next 9 sts, pc, dc in each of next 3 sts; repeat between **], repeat between **], for **Pattern Repeat B,** (skip next 2 sts, dc in each of next 2 sts; working in front of sts just made, tr fp around each of 2 skipped sts, skip next 2 sts, tr fp around each of next 2 sts; working behind sts just made, dc in each of 2 skipped sts) 9 times; repeat between [ ], dc in last st, turn.

Row 22: Repeat row 6.

Row 23: Ch 3, [*dc bp around each of next 2 sts, skip next st, tr fp around next st; working in front of fp just made, tr fp around skipped st, dc bp around each of next 2 sts*, dc in next st, pc, (dc in next 6 sts, pc) 2 times, dc in next st; repeat between **], for **Pattern Repeat A,** (skip next 2 sts, tr fp around each of next 2 sts; working behind sts just made, dc in each of 2 skipped sts, skip next 2 sts, dc in each of next 2 sts; working in front of sts just made, tr fp around 2 skipped sts) 9 times; repeat between [ ], dc in last st, turn.

Row 24: Repeat row 4.

Row 25: Repeat row 21.

Row 26: Repeat row 6.

Row 27: Repeat row 19.

Row 28: Repeat row 4.

Row 29: Repeat row 17.

Row 30: Repeat row 6.

Row 31: Repeat row 15.

Row 32: Repeat row 4.

Rows 33-38: Repeat rows 17-22.

Row 39: Ch 3, [*dc bp around each of next 2 sts, skip next st, tr fp around next st; working in front of fp just made, tr fp around skipped st, dc bp around each of next 2 sts*, dc in next st, pc, dc in next 13 sts, pc, dc in next st; repeat between **], for **Pattern Repeat A,** (skip next 2 sts, tr fp around each of next 2 sts; working behind sts just made, dc in each of 2 skipped sts, skip next 2 sts, dc in each of next 2 sts; working in front of sts just made, tr fp around 2 skipped sts) 9 times; repeat between [ ], dc in last st, turn.

Row 40: Repeat row 4.

Row 41: Ch 3, [*dc bp around each of next 2 sts, skip next st, tr fp around next st; working in front of fp just made, tr fp around skipped st, dc bp around each of next 2 sts*, dc in each of next 2 sts, pc, (dc in next 5 sts, pc) 2 times, dc in each of next 2 sts; repeat between **], for **Pattern Repeat B,** (skip next 2 sts, dc in each of next 2 sts; working in front of sts just made, tr fp around each of 2 skipped sts, skip next 2 sts, tr fp around each of next 2 sts; working behind sts just made, dc in each of 2 skipped sts) 9 times; repeat between [ ], dc in last st, turn.

Row 42: Repeat row 6.

Row 43: Repeat row 19.

Row 44: Repeat row 4.

Row 45: Ch 3, [*dc bp around each of next 2 sts, skip next st, tr fp around next st; working in front of fp just made, tr fp around skipped st, dc bp around each of next 2 sts*, dc in next 17 sts; repeat between **], for **Pattern Repeat B,** (skip next 2 sts, dc in each of next 2 sts; working in front of sts just made, tr fp around each of 2 skipped sts, skip next 2 sts, tr fp around each of next 2 sts; working behind sts just made, dc in each of 2 skipped sts) 9 times; repeat between [ ], dc in last st, turn.

Row 46: Repeat row 6.

Rows 47-52: Repeat rows 3-8.

Row 53: Ch 3, [*dc bp around each of next 2 sts, skip next st, tr fp around next st; working in front of fp just made, tr fp around skipped st, dc bp around each of next 2 sts*, dc in next st, pc, (dc in next 6 sts, pc) 2 times, dc in next st; repeat between **], for **Pattern Repeat B,** (skip next 2 sts, dc in each of next 2 sts; working in front of sts just made, tr fp around each of 2 skipped sts, skip next 2 sts, tr fp around each of next 2 sts; working behind sts just made, dc in each of 2 skipped sts) 9 times; repeat between [ ], dc in last st, turn.

Rows 54-55: Repeat rows 6 and 7.

Rows 56-58: Repeat rows 4-6.

Rows 59-60: Repeat rows 3 and 4.

Row 61: Repeat row 45.

Row 62: Repeat row 6.

Rows 63-84: Repeat rows 3-24.

Row 85: Repeat row 21.

Row 86: Repeat row 6.

Row 87: Repeat row 19.

Row 88: Repeat row 4.

Row 89: Repeat row 17.

Row 90: Repeat row 6.

Rows 91-98: Repeat rows 15-22.

Rows 99-102: Repeat rows 39-42.

Row 103: Repeat row 19.

Row 104: Repeat row 4, **do not** fasten off.

BORDER

Rnd 1: Working around outer edge, ch 1, 3 sc in first st, *sc in next 5 sts, (skip next st, sc in next 4 sts) across to last st, 3 sc in last st; working in ends of rows, sc in first row, 2 sc in next row, (sc in next row, 2 sc in each of next 2 rows) across to next corner*; working in starting ch on opposite side on row 1, 3 sc in first ch; repeat between **, join with sl st in first sc (105 sc across each short end between 3-sc corners, 173 sc across each long edge between 3-sc corners).

Rnd 2: Sl st in next st, ch 4, 5 tr in same st, *sc in next st, skip next st, 5 tr in next st, skip next st, sc in next st, (skip next 2 sts, 5 tr in next st, skip next 2 sts, sc in next st) across to center st of next 3-sc corner group, 6 tr in next st, sc in next st, (skip next 2 sts, 5 tr in next st, skip next 2 sts, sc in next st) across to center st of next 3-sc corner group*, 6 tr in next st; repeat between **, join with sl st in top of ch-4.

Rnd 3: Ch 1, (sc, ch 3, sc) in same st, (sc, ch 3, sc) in each tr and pc in each sc around, join with sl st in first sc, fasten off.✣

Baby's Lullaby

Designer: Rosetta Harshman

Size: 29" x 41" not including Fringe.

Materials: Pompadour baby yarn — 18 oz. white and 12 oz. variegated; tapestry needle; F crochet hook or size needed to obtain gauge.

Gauge: Rnds 1-2 of Motif = 3" across. Each Motif measures 4½" across.

Skill Level: ★★ Average

INSTRUCTIONS

MOTIF (make 60)

Rnd 1: With variegated, ch 7, sl st in first ch to form ring, ch 3, 17 dc in ring, join with sl st in top of ch-3 (18 dc).

NOTES: For **beginning popcorn (beg pc),** ch 3, 3 dc in same st, drop lp from hook, insert hook in top of ch-3, draw dropped lp through, ch 1.

For **popcorn (pc),** 4 dc in next st, drop lp from hook, insert hook in first st of 4-dc group, draw dropped lp through, ch 1.

Rnd 2: Beg pc, ch 3, pc in next st, dc in next st, (pc in next st, ch 3, pc in next st, dc in next st) around, join with sl st in top of beg pc (12 pc, 6 dc, 6 ch sps).

Rnd 3: Ch 3, (pc, ch 3, pc) in next ch sp, dc in next st, 3 dc in next st, *dc in next st, (pc, ch 3, pc) in next ch sp, dc in next st, 3 dc in next st; repeat from * around, join with sl st in top of ch-3, fasten off (30 dc, 12 pc, 6 ch sps).

Rnd 4: Join white with sc in any ch sp, (2 sc, ch 1, 3 sc) in same sp, sc in next 7 sts, *(3 sc, ch 1, 3 sc) in next ch sp, sc in next 7 sts; repeat from * around, join with sl st in first sc, fasten off (78 sc, 6 ch-1 sps).

With white, sew Motifs together through **back lps** according to Assembly Diagram.

EDGING

Working around entire outer edge, with right side facing you, join white with sc in any st, sc in each st, in each ch-1 sp and in each seam around, join with sl st in first sc, fasten off.

FRINGE

For **each Fringe,** cut 3 strands white each 12" long. Holding all strands together, fold in half, insert hook in st, draw fold through, draw all loose ends through fold, tighten. Trim ends.

Fringe in every other st of Edging around Afghan.✣

ASSEMBLY DIAGRAM

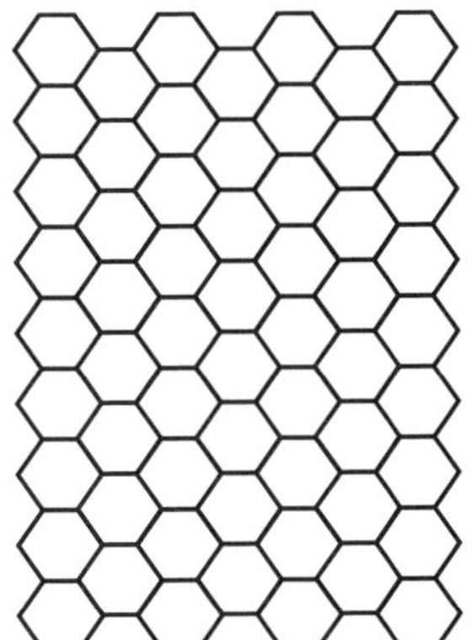

Precious Beginnings

Designer: Jeannine LaRoche

Size: 33" x 46".

Materials: 2-ply baby yarn — 14 oz. each blue, pink and blue/pink/white variegated; tapestry needle; F crochet hook or size needed to obtain gauge.

Gauge: Rnds 1-3 of Block = 2¾" across. Each Block is 6¼" square.

Skill Level: ★★★ Advanced

INSTRUCTIONS

BLOCK (make 35)

Rnd 1: With variegated, ch 6, sl st in first ch to form ring, ch 6, (3 dc in ring, ch 3) 3 times, 2 dc in ring, join with sl st in 3rd ch of ch-6 (12 dc, 4 ch sps).

NOTES: For **long double crochet (ldc),** working over sts, yo, insert hook in ch sp on rnd before last, yo, draw up long lp, (yo, draw through 2 lps on hook) 2 times.

For **double crochet front post (dc fp),** yo, insert hook from front to back around post of next st on rnd before last, yo, draw lp through, (yo, draw through 2 lps on hook) 2 times.

Rnd 2: Sl st in first ch sp, ch 6, dc in same sp, *[ldc in ring, dc in same sp as last dc on this rnd, skip next 3 sts], dc in next ch sp, ldc in ring, (dc, ch 3, dc) in same sp as last dc on this rnd; repeat from * 2 more times; repeat between [ ], dc in same sp as first sl st, ldc in ring, join (16 dc, 8 ldc, 4 ch sps).

Rnd 3: Sl st in first ch sp, ch 6, dc in same sp, ldc in next ch sp on rnd before last, *[dc in same sp as last dc on this rnd, skip next 3 sts, dc in sp between last st and next st, dc fp around 2nd dc of 3-dc group on rnd before last, dc in same sp as last dc on this rnd, skip next 3 sts], dc in next ch sp, ldc in next ch sp on rnd before last, (dc, ch 3, dc) in same sp as last dc on this rnd, ldc in same sp on rnd before last as last ldc; repeat from * 2 more times; repeat between [ ], dc in same sp as first sl st, ldc in next ch sp on rnd before last, join, fasten off.

Rnd 4: Join pink with sl st in first ch sp, ch 6, dc in same sp, ldc in next ch sp on rnd before last, *[dc in same sp as last dc on this rnd, skip next 3 sts, (dc in sp between last dc and next dc, dc fp around ldc on rnd before last, dc in same sp as last dc, skip next 3 sts) across to next ch sp], dc in next ch sp, ldc in next ch sp on rnd before last, (dc, ch 3, dc) in same sp as last dc on this rnd, ldc in same sp on rnd before last as last ldc; repeat from * 2 more times; repeat between [ ], dc in same sp as first sl st, ldc in next ch sp on rnd before last, join.

Rnd 5: Sl st in first ch sp, ch 6, dc in same sp, ldc in next ch sp on rnd before last, *[dc in same sp as last dc on this rnd, skip next 3 sts, (dc in sp between last dc and next dc, dc fp around next ldc or dc fp on rnd before last, dc in same sp as last dc, skip next 3 sts) across to next ch sp], dc in next ch sp, ldc in next ch sp on rnd before last, (dc, ch 3, dc) in same sp as last dc on this rnd, ldc in same sp on rnd before last as last ldc; repeat from * 2 more times; repeat between [ ], dc in same sp as first sl st, ldc in next ch sp on rnd before last, join, fasten off.

Rnds 6-7: With blue, repeat rnds 4 and 5.

Rnd 8: With variegated, repeat rnd 4, fasten off (24 sts across each side between corner ch sps).

Matching sts, sew Blocks together in 5 rows of 7 Blocks each.

BORDER

Rnd 1: Working around outer edge, with right side facing you, join variegated with sc in any corner ch sp, 2 sc in same sp, ◊[(skip next st, sc in each of next 3 sts) 6 times, *sc in next ch sp, skip next seam, sc in next ch sp, (skip next st, sc in each of next 3 sts) 6 times; repeat from * across to next corner ch sp], 3 sc in next corner ch sp; repeat from ◊ 2 more times; repeat between [ ], join with sl st in first sc, **turn.**

NOTE: For **single crochet front post (sc fp),** insert hook from front to back around post of next st, yo, draw lp through, yo, draw through both lps on hook.

Rnd 2: Ch 1, sc fp around each st around, join, **turn,** fasten off.

Rnd 3: Join pink with sc in any st, sc in each st around with 2 sc in each of 3 sc at each corner, join, **turn.**

Rnd 4: Repeat rnd 2.

Rnds 5-6: With blue, repeat rnds 3 and 2.✣

BETSY BEET

Tranquil Ripple

Designer: *Maria Nagy*

Size: 38" square.

Materials: Worsted-weight yarn — 17 oz. white and 12 oz. pink/blue/green ombre; I crochet hook or size needed to obtain gauge.

Gauge: 3 sts = 1"; 3 dc rows = 2".

Skill Level: ★ Easy

INSTRUCTIONS

AFGHAN

Row 1: With white, ch 131, dc in 4th ch from hook, dc in each of next 2 chs, 3 dc in next ch, dc in next 4 chs, (skip next 3 chs, dc in next 4 chs, 3 dc in next ch, dc in next 4 chs) across, turn (121 dc).

Rows 2-3: Working these rows in **back lps** only, ch 3, skip next st, dc in each of next 3 sts, 3 dc in next st, (dc in next 4 sts, skip next 2 sts, dc in next 4 sts, 3 dc in next st) across to last 5 sts, dc in each of next 3 sts, skip next st, dc in last st, turn. At end of last row, fasten off.

Row 4: Working in **both lps,** join ombre with sl st in first st, ch 2, skip next st, hdc in each of next 3 sts, 3 hdc in next st, (hdc in next 4 sts, skip next 2 sts, hdc in next 4 sts, 3 hdc in next st) across to last 5 sts, hdc in each of next 3 sts, skip next st, hdc in last st, turn.

Rows 5-6: Ch 2, skip next st, hdc in each of next 3 sts, 3 hdc in next st, (hdc in next 4 sts, skip next 2 sts, hdc in next 4 sts, 3 hdc in next st) across to last 5 sts, hdc in each of next 3 sts, skip next st, hdc in last st, turn. At end of last row, fasten off.

Row 7: Working in **back lps** only, join white with sl st in first st, ch 3, skip next st, dc in each of next 3 sts, 3 dc in next st, (dc in next 4 sts, skip next 2 sts, dc in next 4 sts, 3 dc in next st) across to last 5 sts, dc in each of next 3 sts, skip next st, dc in last st, turn.

Rows 8-57: Repeat rows 2-7 consecutively, ending with row 3.

Row 58: For **first side,** working in ends of rows, with right side facing you, join white with sl st in end of row 1, ch 3, 2 dc in same row, 3 dc in end of each dc row and 2 dc in end of each hdc row across, turn.

Row 59: Ch 2, skip next st, hdc in each st across, turn.

Row 60: Working this row in **back lps** only, repeat row 59.

Row 61: Working in **both lps,** repeat row 59, fasten off.

For **2nd side,** working in ends of rows on opposite side, joining in end of last row, repeat rows 58-61.✣

SUPPLEMENTARY READERS
THE PLAYTIME PRIMER
CATHERINE T. BRYCE

Sweet & Cuddly

Size: 33" x 41½".

Materials: Fuzzy worsted-weight yarn — 21 oz. pastel ombre; J crochet hook or size needed to obtain gauge.

Gauge: 2 shells and 2 sc = 3½"; 2 shell rows and 2 sc rows = 2¼".

Skill Level: ★ Easy

Designer: Aline Suplinskas

INSTRUCTIONS

AFGHAN

NOTES: For **shell,** 5 dc in next ch or st.

For **reverse shell,** (yo, insert hook in next st, yo, draw lp through, yo, draw through 2 lps on hook) 5 times, yo, draw through all 6 lps on hook.

Row 1: Ch 112, 2 dc in 4th ch from hook, skip next 2 chs, sc in next ch, skip next 2 chs, (shell in next ch, skip next 2 chs, sc in next ch, skip next 2 chs) across to last ch, 3 dc in last ch, turn (18 sc, 17 shells, 6 dc).

Row 2: Ch 1, sc in first st, (ch 2, reverse shell, ch 2, sc in next st) across, turn (37 sts, 36 ch sps).

Row 3: Ch 3, 2 dc in same st, skip next ch sp, sc in next st, skip next ch sp, (shell in next st, skip next ch sp, sc in next st, skip next ch sp) across to last st, 3 dc in last st, turn.

Rows 4-70: Repeat rows 2 and 3 alternately, ending with row 2. At end of last row, **do not** fasten off.

BORDER

NOTE: Work loosely on next rnd. If necessary, to keep work from puckering, use next larger size hook.

Working around outer edge, with right side facing you, ch 3, 7 dc in same st, *skip next ch sp, sc in next st, skip next ch sp, (shell in next st, skip next ch sp, sc in next st, skip next ch sp) across to last st, 8 dc in last st; working in ends of rows, sc in next dc row, (skip next sc row, shell in next dc row, skip next sc row, sc in next dc row) across to next corner*; working in starting ch on opposite side of row 1, 8 dc in first ch; repeat between **, join with sl st in top of ch-3, fasten off.✣

Photo by Mary Van de Ven, Hawaii

Celestial
* Light *

"…There was a time when meadow, grove, and stream,
The earth, and every common sight,
To me did seem
Apparelled in celestial light,
The glory and the freshness of a dream. …"

—William Wordsworth

Heavenly Luster

Designer: Debra Caldwell

Size: 43" x 62".

Materials: Worsted-weight yarn — 50 oz. white with glitter wrap; adjustable hairpin lace loom; G crochet hook or size needed to obtain gauge.

Gauge: 17 dc = 4"; 5 sc rows and 4 dc rows worked in pattern = 3".

Skill Level: ★★★★ Challenging

INSTRUCTIONS

LACE PANEL (make 9)

1: Position loom prongs 2" apart. Remove top bar and slide slip knot lp over left prong. Replace top bar and adjust lp so slip knot is centered between the prongs and yarn held in front of loom (see illustration 1).

2: Wrap yarn from front to back around right prong and hold in place with left hand. Insert hook in lp on left prong as shown in illustration 2. Draw yarn held in back of loom through lp to form a lp on hook.

3: Yo, draw through lp on hook (see illustration 3).

4: Drop lp from hook. From the back of loom, insert hook in dropped lp. Turn loom from right to left in front of you to reverse the position of the prongs.

5: Turning the loom also causes the yarn to wrap around what is now the right prong, thus forming another loop. The crochet hook is now, again, positioned in front of the loom.

6: Insert hook in front strand of lp on left prong, yo, draw yarn through lp (now there are 2 lps on hook) (see illustration 4).

7: Yo, draw through 2 lps on hook (one sc complete).

8: Repeat steps 4-7 81 more times for a total of 82 sc between lps. Each new lp is formed by turning the loom after completing a sc between the prongs. When loom becomes full, remove bottom bar and take off all but the last 4-6 lps (see illustration 5). Replace bottom bar to continue work.

Edging

Working across one long edge of Panel, with all lps of Panel folded right over left, with crochet hook, join with sc in first lp, (ch 1, sc in next lp) across, fasten off (82 sc, 81 ch-1 sps).

Repeat on opposite edge.

HAIRPIN LACE ILLUSTRATION

1

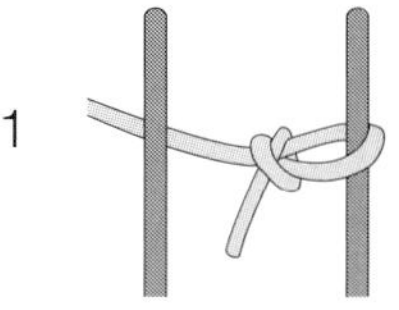

3

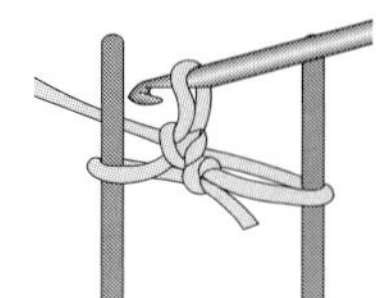

2

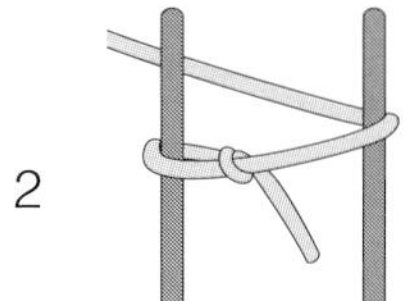

4

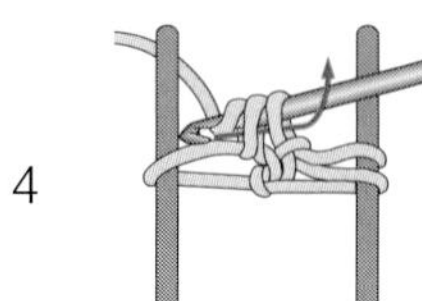

5

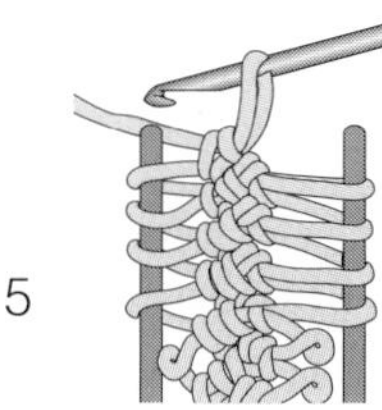

DIAMOND PANEL (make 10)

Row 1: With crochet hook, ch 164, sc in 2nd ch from hook, sc in each ch across, turn (163 sc).

Row 2: Ch 3, dc in each st across, turn.

NOTES: For **beginning half diamond (beg half diamond),** yo 2 times, insert hook from front to back around post of 4th st on row before last, yo, draw lp through, (yo, draw through 2 lps on hook) 3 times, skip next st on last row behind beg half diamond.

For **ending half diamond (end half diamond),** yo 2 times, insert hook from front to back around post of same st as 2nd half of last diamond made, yo, draw lp through, (yo, draw through 2 lps

Continued on page 111

Galaxy Glimmer

Designer: Sandra Smith

Size: 45½" x 68" not including Tassels.

Materials: Worsted-weight yarn — 49 oz. berry and 21½ oz. white; tapestry needle; G crochet hook or size needed to obtain gauge.

Gauge: Rnds 1-3 of Motif = 3½" across. Each Cross and Motif = 7½" across.

Skill Level: ★★★ Advanced

INSTRUCTIONS

STAR STRIP (make 5)

First Star

Rnd 1: With berry, ch 6, sl st in first ch to form ring, ch 1, 16 sc in ring, join with sl st in first sc (16 sc).

Rnd 2: Working this rnd in **back lps** only, ch 6, skip next st, (dc in next st, ch 3, skip next st) around, join with sl st in 3rd ch of ch-6 (8 dc, 8 ch-3 sps).

Rnd 3: Ch 3, 4 dc in next ch sp, (dc in next st, 4 dc in next ch sp) around, join with sl st in top of ch-3 (40 dc).

NOTES: For **beginning shell (beg shell),** ch 3, (3 dc, ch 2, 4 dc) in same st or sp.

For **shell,** (4 dc, ch 2, 4 dc) in next st or ch sp.

Rnd 4: Beg shell, skip next 4 sts, (shell in next st, skip next 4 sts) around, join (8 shells).

Rnd 5: Sl st in each of next 3 sts, sl st in next ch sp, ch 1, sc in same sp, shell in sp between same shell and next shell, (sc in ch sp of next shell, shell in sp between same shell and next shell) around, join with sl st in first sc (8 sc, 8 shells).

Rnd 6: Skip first st, *[sc in next 4 sts, (2 sc, ch 2, 2 sc) in next ch sp, sc in next 4 sts], sl st in next st; repeat from * 6 more times; repeat between [ ], join with sl st in joining sl st on last rnd, fasten off (96 sc, 8 ch-2 sps, 8 sl sts).

Next Star

Rnds 1-5: Repeat same rnds of First Motif.

Rnd 6: Skip first st, *[sc in next 4 sts, (2 sc, ch 2, 2 sc) in next ch sp, sc in next 4 sts], sl st in next st; repeat from * 5 more times, sc in next 4 sts, 2 sc in next ch sp, ch 1, sl st in top center ch sp on last Motif made, ch 1, 2 sc in same sp on this Motif, sc in next 4 sts, sl st in next st; repeat between [ ], join with sl st in joining sl st on last rnd, fasten off.

Repeat Next Star 6 more times for a total of 8 Stars in Strip.

CROSS STRIP (make 6)

First Cross

Rnd 1: With white, ch 6, sl st in first ch to form ring, ch 1, 16 sc in ring, join with sl st in first sc, fasten off (16 sc).

Rnd 2: Working this rnd in **back lps** only, join berry with sl st in any st, *[ch 8, dc in 4th ch from hook, ch 2, skip next 2 chs, dc in each of next 2 chs, skip next sc], sl st in each of next 3 sc; repeat from * 2 more times; repeat between [ ], sl st in each of last 2 sc, join with sl st in first sl st (12 dc, 12 sl sts, 4 ch-3 sps, 4 ch-2 sps).

Rnd 3: Working on opposite side of chs on first arm of Cross, sl st in first ch, ch 1, sc in same ch, sc in next ch, *[2 sc in next ch sp, sc in next ch, (3 sc, ch 2, 3 sc) in ch-3 sp at end of arm, sc in next dc, 2 sc in next ch sp, sc in each of next 2 dc, skip next sl st, sl st in next sl st, skip next sl st], sc in each of next 2 chs; repeat from * 2 more times; repeat between [ ], join with sl st in first sc, fasten off (64 sc, 4 sl sts, 4 ch-2 sps).

Rnd 4: Working this rnd in **back lps** only, join white with sl st in first ch of any ch-2, ch 3, dc in same ch, *[ch 2, 2 dc in next ch, dc in each of next 2 sts, (dc, ch 2, dc) in next st, dc in next 4 sts; skipping sl st between arms of Cross, dc next 2 sc tog, dc in next 4 sts, (dc, ch 2, dc) in next st, dc in each of next 2 sts], 2 dc in next ch; repeat from * 2 more times; repeat between [ ], join with sl st in top of ch-3, fasten off (84 dc, 12 ch-2 sps).

Next Cross

Rnds 1-3: Repeat same rnds of First Cross.

Rnd 4: Working this rnd in **back lps** only, join white with sl st in first ch of any ch-2, ch 3, dc in

Continued on page 110

Jason

Midnight Glow

Designer: Roberta Maier

Size: 55" x 77".

Materials: Worsted-weight yarn — 43 oz. black and 32½ oz. off-white; I crochet hook or size needed to obtain gauge.

Gauge: 3 dc = 1"; Rnds 1-3 of Block = 3¾" across. Each Block is 10¾" square.

Skill Level: ★★ Average

INSTRUCTIONS

FIRST ROW

First Block

Rnd 1: With off-white, ch 4, sl st in first ch to form ring, ch 5, (3 dc in ring, ch 2) 3 times, 2 dc in ring, join with sl st in 3rd ch of ch-5 (12 dc, 4 ch-2 sps).

NOTES: For **treble crochet front post stitch (fp),** yo 2 times, insert hook from front to back around post of next st (see figure 9, page 159), yo, draw lp through, (yo, draw through 2 lps on hook) 3 times.

For **beginning shell (beg shell),** ch 3, (dc, ch 1, 2 dc) in same sp.

For **shell,** (2 dc, ch 1, 2 dc) in next ch sp.

For **beginning V-stitch (beg V-st),** ch 4, dc in same sp.

For **V-stitch (V-st),** (dc, ch 1, dc) in next ch sp.

Rnd 2: Sl st in next ch sp, beg shell, dc in next st, fp, dc in next st, (shell in next ch sp, dc in next st, fp, dc in next st) around, join with sl st in top of ch-3 (8 dc, 4 fp, 4 shells).

Rnd 3: Sl st in next st, sl st in next ch sp, beg V-st, (*dc in each of next 3 sts, fp, dc in each of next 3 sts*, V-st) 3 times; repeat between **, join with sl st in 3rd ch of ch-4, fasten off (24 dc, 4 fp, 4 V-sts).

Rnd 4: Join black with sl st in any ch sp, beg shell, *[fp, (dc in each of next 3 sts, fp) 2 times], shell; repeat from * 2 more times; repeat between [ ], join with sl st in top of ch-3, fasten off.

Rnd 5: Join off-white with sl st in any ch sp, beg V-st, *[dc in each of next 2 sts, fp, (dc in each of next 3 sts, fp) 2 times, dc in each of next 2 sts], V-st; repeat from * 2 more times; repeat between [ ], join with sl st in 3rd ch of ch-4.

Rnd 6: Sl st in next ch sp, beg shell, *[dc in each of next 3 sts, (fp, dc in each of next 3 sts) 3 times], shell; repeat from * 2 more times; repeat between [ ], join with sl st in top of ch-3.

Rnd 7: Sl st in next st, sl st in next ch sp, beg V-st, *[dc in next st, fp, (dc in each of next 3 sts, fp) 4 times, dc in next st], V-st; repeat from * 2 more times; repeat between [ ], join with sl st in 3rd ch of ch-4, fasten off.

Rnd 8: Join black with sl st in any ch sp, beg shell, *[dc in each of next 2 sts, fp, (dc in each of next 3 sts, fp) 4 times, dc in each of next 2 sts], shell; repeat from * 2 more times; repeat between [ ], join with sl st in top of ch-3.

Rnd 9: Ch 1, sc in each st around with (sc, ch 1, sc) in each corner ch sp, join with sl st in first sc (108 sc, 4 ch-1 sps).

Rnd 10: Sl st in next st, ch 1, sc in same st, ch 3, skip next st, *[(sc, ch 5, sc) in next corner ch sp, ch 3, skip next st, (sc in next st, ch 3, skip next st) across] to next corner ch sp; repeat from * 2 more times; repeat between [ ], join, fasten off.

Second Block

Rnds 1-9: Repeat same rnds of First Block.

NOTES: For **joining ch-3 sp,** ch 1, sc in corresponding ch-3 sp on other Block, ch 1.

For **joining ch-5 sp,** ch 2, sc in corresponding ch-5 sp on other Block, ch 2.

Rnd 10: Sl st in next st, ch 1, sc in same st, ch 3, skip next st, *(sc, ch 5, sc) in next corner ch sp, [ch 3, skip next st, (sc in next st, ch 3, skip next st) across] to next corner ch sp; repeat from *, sc in next corner ch sp; joining to side of last Block made (see Assembly Diagram on page 113), work joining ch-5 sp, sc in same sp on this Block, work joining ch-3 sp, skip next st on this Block, (sc in next st, work joining ch-3 sp, skip next st on this Block) across to next corner ch sp, sc in next ch sp, work joining ch-5 sp, sc in same sp on this Block; repeat between [ ], join, fasten off.

Continued on page 113

Moonbeams

Designer: Rosalie De Vries

Size: 44¾" x 69½".

Materials: Worsted-weight yarn — 22 oz. med. blue, 13 oz. each dk. blue and med. rose, 10 oz. dk. rose and 7 oz. white; tapestry needle; H crochet hook or size needed to obtain gauge.

Gauge: 14 dc = 4"; 5 dc rnds = 3". Block is 12¼" square.

Skill Level: ★★★★ Challenging

INSTRUCTIONS

BLOCK A (make 8)

NOTE: Each ch-3 will be used and counted as a dc.

Rnd 1: With white, ch 4, 2 dc in 4th ch from hook, *[ch 4, (3 dc, ch 3, sl st) in 4th ch from hook], 3 dc in first ch of first ch-4; repeat from * 2 more times; repeat between [ ], join with sl st in top of first ch-4, fasten off (32 dc).

Rnd 2: Join dk. blue with sl st in first st, ch 3, dc in each of next 2 sts, (*sl st in top of next ch-3, ch 3, dc in next st, 5 dc in next st, dc in next st, ch 3, sl st in top of next ch-3*, dc in each of next 3 sts) 3 times; repeat between **, join with sl st in top of ch-3, fasten off (48).

Rnd 3: Join med. blue with sl st in first st, ch 3, dc in each of next 2 sts, (*sl st in next st, ch 3, dc in each of next 3 sts, 5 dc in next st, dc in each of next 3 sts, ch 3, sl st in next st*, dc in each of next 3 sts) 3 times; repeat between **, join, fasten off (64).

Rnd 4: Join dk. rose with sl st in first st, ch 3, dc in each of next 2 sts, *[sl st in next st, ch 3, dc in next st, ch 3, sl st in next 4 sts, (sl st, ch 3, 3 dc, ch 3, sl st) in next st, sl st in next 4 sts, ch 3, dc in next st, ch 3, sl st in next st], dc in each of next 3 sts; repeat from * 2 more times; repeat between [ ], join, fasten off (56).

Rnd 5: Join med. rose with sl st in first st, ch 3, dc in each of next 2 sts, *[sl st in next st, ch 3, (dc in next st, ch 3, sl st in next st, dc in each of next 3 sl sts, sl st in next st, ch 3, dc in next st), 5 dc in next st; repeat between ( ), ch 3, sl st in next st], dc in each of next 3 sts; repeat from * 2 more times; repeat between [ ], join, fasten off (96).

Rnd 6: Join white with sl st in first st, ch 3, dc in each of next 2 sts, *[sl st in next st, ch 3, dc in next st, (ch 3, sl st in next st, dc in each of next 3 sts, sl st in next st, ch 3), dc in each of next 3 sts, 5 dc in next st, dc in each of next 3 sts; repeat between ( ), dc in next st, ch 3, sl st in next st], dc in each of next 3 sts; repeat from * 2 more times; repeat between [ ], join, fasten off (112).

Rnd 7: Join dk. blue with sl st in first st, ch 3, dc in each of next 2 sts, ◊[sl st in next st, *ch 3, dc in next st, ch 3, sl st in next st, dc in each of next 3 sts, sl st in next st, ch 3, dc in next st, ch 3*, sl st in next 4 sts, (sl st, ch 3, 3 dc, ch 3, sl st) in next st, sl st in next 4 sts, ch 3, dc in next st, ch 3, sl st in next 4 sts; repeat between **, sl st in next st], dc in each of next 3 sts; repeat from ◊ 2 more times; repeat between [ ], join, fasten off (104).

Rnd 8: Join med. blue with sl st in first st, ch 3, dc in each of next 2 sts, *[(sl st in next st, ch 3, dc in next st, ch 3, sl st in next st, dc in each of next 3 sts) 2 times, sl st in next st, ch 3, dc in next st, 5 dc in next st, dc in next st, ch 3, sl st in next st, (dc in each of next 3 sts, sl st in next st, ch 3, dc in next st, ch 3, sl st in next st) 2 times], dc in each of next 3 sts; repeat from * 2 more times; repeat between [ ], join, fasten off (144).

Rnd 9: Join dk. blue with sl st in first st, ch 3, dc in each of next 2 sts, *[(sl st in next st, ch 3, dc in next st, ch 3, sl st in next st, dc in each of next 3 sts) 2 times, sl st in next st, ch 3, dc in each of next 3 sts, 5 dc in next st, dc in each of next 3 sts, ch 3, sl st in next st, (dc in each of next 3 sts, sl st in next st, ch 3, dc in next st, ch 3, sl st in next st) 2 times], dc in each of next 3 sts; repeat from * 2 more times; repeat between [ ], join, fasten off (160).

Rnd 10: Join med. blue with sl st in first st, ch 4, tr in each of next 2 sts, *[(sc in each of next 3 sts, tr in each of next 3 sts) 2 times, sc in next 6 sts, (2 sc, hdc, 2 sc) in next st, sc in next 6 sts, (tr in each of next 3 sts, sc in each of next 3 sts) 2 times], tr in each of next 3 sts; repeat from * 2 more times; repeat between [ ], join with sl st in top of ch-4, fasten off (176 sts).

BLOCK B (make 7)

Rnds 1-9: Reversing shades of blue and rose (see photo), repeat same rnds of Block A.

Continued on page 112

Northern Lights

Designer: Darla J. Fanton

Size: 55" x 70".

Materials: Worsted-weight yarn — 27½ oz. each colonial blue and black, 24 oz. scrap yarn in assorted colors (each "block" will require approximately 10 yds. each of 2 colors of scrap yarn); tapestry needle; H crochet hook or size needed to obtain gauge.

Gauge: 10 hdc = 3"; 10 hdc rows = 3".

Skill Level: ★★ Average

INSTRUCTIONS

STRIP (make 7)

NOTES: When changing colors (see illustration on page 159), always drop yarn to wrong side of work. Use a separate skein or ball of yarn for each color section. **Do not** carry yarn across from one section to another. Fasten off colors at end of each color section.

Each square on graph equals one hdc.

Beginning ch-2 is used and counted as first st of each row.

Work odd-numbered graph rows from right to left and even-numbered rows from left to right.

Row 1: With blue, ch 26, hdc in 3rd ch from hook, hdc in each ch across, turn (25 hdc). Front of row 1 is right side of work.

Row 2: Ch 2, hdc in each st across, turn.

Row 3: For row 3 of graph, working under both top lps and **back bar of hdc** (see illustration), ch 2, hdc in next st changing to black (see Notes), hdc in next 10 sts changing to scrap yarn, hdc in next st changing to black, hdc in next 10 sts changing to colonial blue, hdc in last st, turn.

NOTE: Work all hdc of remaining even-numbered rows in top two lps as you would normally. Work all hdc in remaining odd-numbered rows going under top lps and back bars. This will eliminate the pronounced ridge usually seen on the back side of a hdc row.

Rows 4-25: Ch 2, hdc in each st across changing colors according to corresponding row on graph, turn.

Rows 26-225: Repeating rows 1-25 of graph consecutively, ch 2, hdc in each st across changing colors according to graph, turn. At end of last row, fasten off.

Matching ends of rows, with blue, sew Strips together.

BORDER

Rnd 1: Working around outer edge, join blue with sl st in any st, ch 2, hdc in each st, in each seam and in ends of each row around with 3 hdc in each corner, join with sl st in top of ch-2.

Rnd 2: Ch 2, hdc in each st around with 3 hdc in each center corner st, join, fasten off.

Rnd 3: Join black with sc in any st, sc in each st around with 3 sc in each center corner st, join with sl st in first sc, fasten off.

Rnd 4: With blue, repeat rnd 3.✣

BACK BAR OF HDC

HALF DOUBLE CROCHET/ COLOR CHANGE

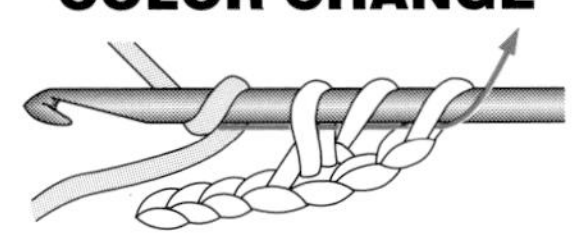

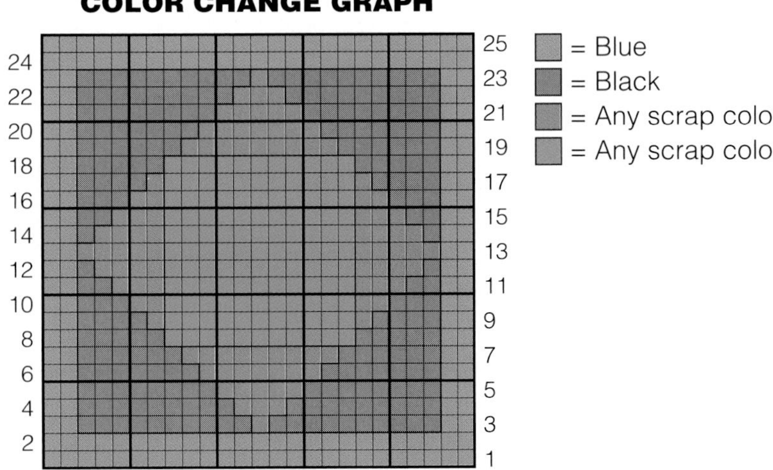

Spinning Stars

Size: 44" x $69\frac{1}{2}$".

Materials: Worsted-weight yarn — 18 oz. med. aqua, 14 oz. gold, 12 oz. each black and dk. aqua, 5 oz. white; tapestry needle; G crochet hook or size needed to obtain gauge.

Gauge: 15 sc = 4"; Rnds 1-2 = $3\frac{1}{2}$" across. Block is $8\frac{1}{2}$" square.

Skill Level: ★★★ Advanced

Designer: Rosalie De Vries

INSTRUCTIONS

BLOCK (make 40)

NOTE: Each ch-3 will be used and counted as a dc.

Rnd 1: With dk. aqua, ch 5, (dc, ch 3, sl st) in 4th ch from hook, sc in next ch, *ch 4, (dc, ch 3, sl st) in 4th ch from hook, sc in same ch as last sc; repeat from * 2 more times, join with sl st in same ch as first dc, fasten off (12 dc, 4 sc).

Rnd 2: Join white with sl st in any sc, ch 8, *[(dc, ch 3, sl st) in 4th ch from hook, tr in same sc, sc in next dc, (sl st, ch 3, dc, ch 3, sl st) in next dc, sc in next dc], tr in next sc, ch 4; repeat from * 2 more times; repeat between [ ], join with sl st in 4th of ch-8, fasten off (24 dc, 8 sc, 8 tr).

Rnd 3: Join gold with sl st in any sc, ch 8, *[(dc, ch 3, sl st) in 4th ch from hook, tr in same sc, sc in next dc, (sl st, ch 3, dc, ch 3, sl st) in next dc, sc in next dc], tr in next sc, ch 4; repeat from * 6 more times; repeat between [ ], join, fasten off (48 dc, 16 sc, 16 tr).

Rnd 4: Join dk. aqua with sl st in any sc, ch 8, *[(dc, ch 3, sl st) in 4th ch from hook, sc in each of next 3 dc], tr in next sc, ch 4; repeat from * 14 more times; repeat between [ ], join, fasten off (48 dc, 48 sc, 16 tr).

Rnd 5: Join med. aqua with sl st in center sc of any 3-sc group, ch 8, *[(dc, ch 3, sl st) in 4th ch from hook, tr in same sc, skip next sc, sc in each of next 3 dc, (tr in each of next 3 sc, sc in each of next 3 dc) 3 times, skip next sc], tr in next sc, ch 4; repeat from * 2 more times; repeat between [ ], join, fasten off (48 sc, 44 tr, 12 dc).

Rnd 6: Join black with sl st in first dc, ch 2, hdc in same st, *[(hdc, dc, hdc) in next dc, 2 hdc in next dc, tr in each of next 2 sc, skip next tr, dc in each of next 3 sts, hdc in each of next 3 sts, sc in next 5 sts, hdc in each of next 3 sts, dc in each of next 3 sts, tr in each of next 2 sts, skip next tr], 2 hdc in next dc; repeat from * 2 more times; repeat between [ ], join with sl st in top of ch-2, fasten off (112 sts).

Rnd 7: Join gold with sc in any st, sc in each st around with (sc, hdc, sc) in each center corner st, join with sl st in first sc, fasten off (120 sts).

Rnd 8: With med. aqua, repeat rnd 7 (128 sts).

Matching sts, with med. aqua, sew Blocks together in five rows of eight Blocks each.

BORDER

Rnd 1: Working around outer edge, join black with sc in any st, sc in each st and in each seam around with (sc, hdc, sc) in each center corner st, join with sl st in first sc, fasten off.

Rnd 2: Join med. aqua with sc in any st, sc in each st around with (sc, hdc, sc) in each center corner st, join, **turn,** fasten off.

Rnd 3: Join gold with sl st in any st; for **reverse sc,** working from left to right, insert hook in next st, yo, draw lp through, yo, draw through both lps on hook; reverse sc in each st around, join, fasten off.✣

Today
STAR

Galaxy Glimmer

continued from page 100

same ch, *◊ch 2, 2 dc in next ch, [dc in each of next 2 sts, (dc, ch 2, dc) in next dc, dc in next 4 sts; skipping sl st between arms of Cross, dc next 2 sc tog, dc in next 4 sts, (dc, ch 2, dc) in next st, dc in each of next 2 sts◊, 2 dc in next ch]; repeat from *, ch 1, sl st in ch-2 sp of top arm on last Cross made, ch 1, 2 dc in next ch on this Cross; repeat between [ ]; repeat between ◊◊, join with sl st in top of ch-3, fasten off.

Repeat Next Cross seven more times for a total of nine Crosses in Strip.

ASSEMBLY

Holding Strips wrong sides together, matching sts, with berry, sl st Strips together through **back lps** only as shown in Assembly Diagram.

EDGING

NOTES: For **tassel,** (ch 10, sl st in 2nd ch from hook, sl st in next 8 chs) 4 times, sl st in next ch of ch-2 on Cross.

For **sl st decrease (dec),** insert hook in next st or ch, yo, draw lp through, skip next st or ch, insert hook in next st or ch, yo, draw lp through st and both lps on hook.

Working around entire outer edge in **back lps** only, join berry with sl st in first ch of any ch-2 at tip of arm indicated on Assembly Diagram; work tassel, sl st in next 11 sts and chs, dec, *sl st in next 12 sts and chs, work tassel, (sl st in next 11 sts and chs, dec) 3 times*; repeat between ** 4 more times, [sl st in next 12 sts and chs, work tassel, sl st in next 11 sts and chs, dec]; repeat between ** 8 times; repeat between [ ]; repeat between ** 5 times; repeat between [ ]; repeat between ** 8 times, sl st in last 11 sts and chs, join with sl st in joining sl st, fasten off.

FINISHING

For each tassel, cut 12" of white, wrap white four times around all four chs held together ½" from edge of Cross; tie ends in knot. Hide ends under wraps and trim excess.

With two 5" pieces of white held together, tie a knot around ch-2 sps between Crosses as shown in diagram.✣

ASSEMBLY DIAGRAM

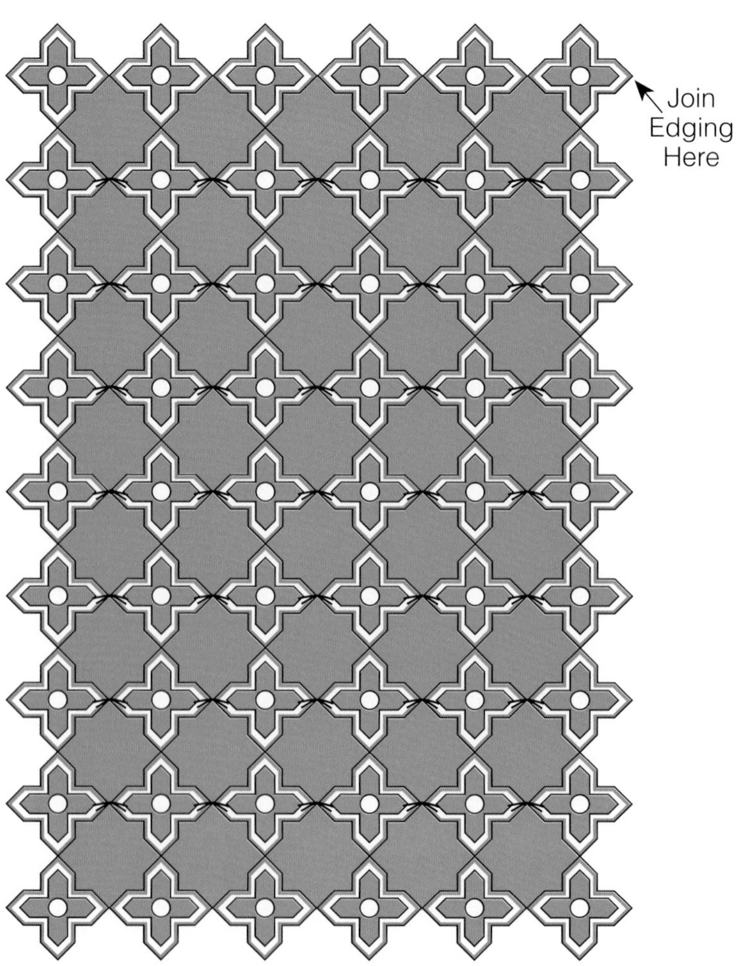

continued from page 99

on hook) 3 times, skip next st on last row behind end half diamond.

For **beginning diamond (beg diamond),** yo 2 times, insert hook from front to back around post of 2nd st on row before last, yo, draw lp through, (yo, draw through 2 lps on hook) 2 times, skip next 3 sts on row before last, yo 2 times, insert hook from front to back around post of next st, yo, draw lp through, (yo, draw through 2 lps on hook) 2 times, yo, draw through all 3 lps on hook, skip next st on last row behind diamond.

For **diamond,** yo 2 times, insert hook from front to back around post of same st on row before last as 2nd half of last diamond made, yo, draw lp through, (yo, draw through 2 lps on hook) 2 times, skip next 3 sts on row before last, yo 2 times, insert hook from front to back around post of next st, yo, draw lp through, (yo, draw through 2 lps on hook) 2 times, yo, draw through all 3 lps on hook, skip next st on last row behind diamond.

Row 3: Ch 1, sc in first st, beg half diamond, sc in each of next 3 sts, (diamond, sc in each of next 3 sts) across to last 2 sts, end half diamond, sc in last st, turn (122 sc, 39 diamonds, 2 half diamonds).

Row 4: Repeat row 2.

Row 5: Ch 1, sc in each of first 3 sts, beg diamond, sc in each of next 3 sts, (diamond, sc in each of next 3 sts) across, turn (123 sc, 40 diamonds).

Rows 6-9: Repeat rows 2-5.

Row 10: Ch 1, sc in each st across, fasten off.

Holding one Diamond Panel and one Lace Panel wrong sides together, matching sts and ch-1 sps on one long edge, join with sl st in first st, sl st in each st across, fasten off.

Starting with Diamond Panel, alternating Lace Panels and Diamond Panels, join remaining Panels in same manner.

BORDER

Rnd 1: Working around entire outer edge, starting on opposite side of row 1 on first Diamond Panel, join with sc in first ch, sc in same ch, sc in each ch across with 3 sc in last ch; [working in ends of rows, sc in next row on Diamond Panel, (2 sc in next row, sc in next row) 4 times, *sc in next row on Lace Panel, ch 4, dc in sc between lps, ch 4, sc in last row on same Panel, sc in next row on Diamond Panel, (2 sc in next row, sc in next row) 4 times; repeat from * 8 more times]; working in sts of last row of last Diamond Panel, 3 sc in first st, sc in each st across with 3 sc in last st; repeat between [ ], sc in same st as first st, join with sl st in first sc (163 sts on each short end between corner sc, 159 sts and 18 ch-4 sps on each long edge between corner sc).

NOTE: For **treble crochet front post stitch (tr fp),** yo 2 times, insert hook from front to back around post of next st on rnd before last (see figure 9, page 159) or around end of row before last rnd, yo, draw lp through, (yo, draw through 2 lps on hook) 3 times, skip next st on last rnd behind tr fp.

Rnd 2: Ch 3, dc in next st; working tr fp around bars between chs on starting ch of Panel, tr fp, (dc in next st, tr fp) across to next 3-sc corner, [dc in each of next 3 sts, tr fp around next row, (dc in next st, tr fp around next row) 6 times, *dc in next st, tr in next ch sp, dc in 2nd ch of same sp, tr in same sp, dc in 4th ch of same sp, tr fp around next dc on last rnd, dc in first ch of next ch sp, tr in same sp, dc in 3rd ch of same sp, tr in same sp, dc in next st, tr fp around next row, (dc in next st, tr fp around next row) 6 times; repeat from * 8 more times], dc in each of next 3 sts, tr fp, (dc in next st, tr fp) across to next 3-sc corner; repeat between [ ], dc in last st, join with sl st in top of ch-3 (163 sts on each short end between corner dc, 231 sts on each long edge between corner dc).

NOTE: Work all remaining tr fp around post of next st on last rnd.

Rnds 3-4: Ch 3, dc in same st, *[tr fp, (dc in next st, tr fp) across to next corner st], 3 dc in next st; repeat from * 2 more times; repeat between [ ], dc in same st as first st, join, ending with 167 sts on each short end between corner dc and 235 sts on each long edge between corner dc in last rnd.

Rnd 5: Ch 1, 2 sc in first st, sc in each st around with 3 sc in each center corner st, sc in same st as first st, join with sl st in first sc (169 sc on each short end between corner sc and 237 sc on each long edge between corner sc).

NOTE: For **scallop,** skip next st, 3 dc in next st; working around last 3 dc made, 3 dc in skipped st.

Rnd 6: Ch 1, sc in first st, skip next st, scallop, skip next st, (sc in next st, skip next st, scallop, skip next st) around to last st, skip last st, join.

Rnd 7: Working in **back lps** only, sl st in each st around, join with sl st in first sl st, fasten off.✣

Moonbeams

continued from page 104

Rnd 10: Repeat same rnd of Block A.

ASSEMBLY

Starting with Block A in any corner, alternating Blocks, with med. blue, sew Blocks together in three rows of five Blocks each, matching sts and sewing from center corner st to center corner st. (There should be 45 sts on edge of each sewn Block.)

BORDER

Rnd 1: Working around outer edge, join white with sl st in center corner st before one short end, ch 3, 4 dc in same st, dc in next st, ◊[*(ch 3, sl st in next 5 sts, ch 3, dc in next st) 7 times, dc in next joined center corner st, dc in joined center corner st on next Block, dc in next st; repeat from * across to last Block on this side; repeat between ( ) 7 more times], 5 dc in next st; repeat from ◊ 2 more times; repeat between [ ], join with sl st in top of ch-3, fasten off (74 dc on each short end between each corner dc, 122 dc on each long edge between corner dc).

Rnd 2: Join dk. rose with sl st in first center corner st, ch 3, 4 dc in same st, ◊dc in each of next 3 sts, *[ch 3, sl st in next st, dc in each of next 3 sl sts, (sl st in next st, ch 3, dc in next st, ch 3, sl st in next st, dc in each of next 3 sl sts) 6 times, sl st in next st, ch 3], dc in next 4 sts*; repeat between **; repeat between [ ], dc in each of next 3 sts, 5 dc in next st, dc in each of next 3 sts; repeat between ** 4 times; repeat between [ ], dc in each of next 3 sts◊, 5 dc in next st; repeat between ◊◊, join, fasten off.

Rnd 3: Join med. rose with sl st in first center corner st, ch 3, 4 dc in same st, [dc in next 5 sts, *(ch 3, sl st in next st, dc in each of next 3 sts, sl st in next st, ch 3, dc in next st) 7 times, dc in each of next 3 sts*; repeat between ** 2 more times, dc in next st, 5 dc in next st, dc in next 5 sts; repeat between ** 5 times, dc in next st], 5 dc in next st; repeat between [ ], join, fasten off.

Rnd 4: Join dk. blue with sl st in first center corner st, ch 3, 4 dc in same st, ◊[dc in next st, ch 3, sl st in next 5 sts, (ch 3, dc in next st, ch 3, sl st in next st, dc in each of next 3 sts, sl st in next st) 7 times, *ch 3, dc in next 4 sts, ch 3, sl st in next st, dc in each of next 3 sts, sl st in next st*; repeat between ( ) 6 times; repeat between **; repeat between ( ) 6 times], ch 3, dc in next st, ch 3, sl st in next 5 sts, ch 3, dc in next st, 5 dc in next center corner st; repeat between [ ]; repeat between **; repeat between ( ) 6 times; repeat between **; repeat between ( ) 6 times, ch 3, dc in next st, ch 3, sl st in next 5 sts, ch 3, dc in next st◊, 5 dc in next center corner st; repeat between ◊◊, join, fasten off.

Rnd 5: Join med. blue with sl st in first center corner st, ch 3, 4 dc in same st, dc in each of next 3 sts, ch 3, sl st in next st, dc in each of next 3 sl sts, sl st in next st, *(ch 3, dc in next st, ch 3, sl st in next st, dc in each of next 3 sts, sl st in next st) across to next 6-dc group, ch 3, dc in next 4 sts, ch 3, sl st in next st, dc in each of next 3 sts, sl st in next st*; repeat between **; [◊repeat between ( ) 6 times, ch 3, dc in next st, ch 3, sl st in next st, dc in each of next 3 sl sts, sl st in next st, ch 3, dc in each of next 3 sts◊, 5 dc in next st, dc in each of next 3 sts, ch 3, sl st in next st, dc in each of next 3 sl sts, sl st in next st]; repeat between ** 4 times; repeat between [ ]; repeat between ** 2 times; repeat between [ ]; repeat between ** 4 times; repeat between ◊◊, join, fasten off.

Rnd 6: Join dk. blue with sl st in first center corner st, ch 3, 4 dc in same st, dc in next 5 sts, ch 3, sl st in next st, dc in each of next 3 sts, *(sl st in next st, ch 3, dc in next st, ch 3, sl st in next st, dc in each of next 3 sts) across to next 6-dc group, sl st in next st, ch 3, dc in next 4 sts, ch 3, sl st in next st, dc in each of next 3 sts*; repeat between **; [◊repeat between ( ) 7 times, sl st in next st, ch 3, dc in next 5 sts◊, 5 dc in next st, dc in next 5 sts, ch 3, sl st in next st, dc in each of next 3 sts]; repeat between ** 4 times; repeat between [ ];

repeat between ** 2 times; repeat between [ ]; repeat between ** 4 times; repeat between ◊◊, join, fasten off.

Rnd 7: Join med. blue with sc in first center corner st, (sc, hdc, 2 sc) in same st, ◊sc in next 8 sts, *tr in each of next 3 sts, (sc in each of next 3 sts, tr in each of next 3 sts) across to next 6-dc group, sc in next 6 sts*; repeat between **, [tr in each of next 3 sts; repeat between ( ) 7 times, sc in next 8 sts, (2 sc, hdc, 2 sc) in next st, sc in next 8 sts]; repeat between ** 4 times; repeat between [ ]; repeat between ** 2 times; repeat between [ ]; repeat between ** 4 times, tr in each of next 3 sts; repeat between ( ) 7 times, sc in last 8 sts, join with sl st in first sc.

Rnd 8: Working this rnd in **back lps** only; for **reverse sc,** working from left to right, insert hook in next st to the right, yo, draw lp through, yo, draw through both lps on hook; reverse sc in each st around, join, **turn,** fasten off.

Rnd 9: With wrong side facing you, join med. blue with sl st around post of any st on last rnd, sl st around post of each st around, join with sl st in first sl st, fasten off.✣

Midnight Glow

continued from page 103

Repeat Second Block three more times for a total of five Blocks.

SECOND ROW

First Block

Joining to bottom of First Block on last Row (see diagram), work same as Second Block on First Row.

Second Block

Rnds 1-9: Repeat same rnds of First Block on First Row.

Rnd 10: Sl st in next st, ch 1, sc in same st, ch 3, skip next st, (sc, ch 5, sc) in next corner ch sp, [ch 3, skip next st, (sc in next st, ch 3, skip next st) across] to next corner ch sp, sc in next ch sp; joining to bottom of next Block on last Row made, work joining ch-5 sp, sc in same sp on this Block, *work joining ch-3 sp, skip next st on this Block, (sc in next st, work joining ch-3 sp, skip next st on this Block) across to next corner ch sp, sc in next ch sp, work joining ch-5 sp, sc in same sp on this Block*; joining to side of last Block on this Row; repeat between **; repeat between [ ], join, fasten off.

Repeat Second Block three more times for a total of five Blocks.

Repeat Second Row five more times for a total of seven Rows.

EDGING

Rnd 1: Join black with sc in 3rd ch of any corner ch-5 sp, ch 5, sc in same ch, ◊[ch 3, (sc in 2nd of ch of next ch-3 sp, ch 3) 14 times, *sc in joining sc, ch 3, skip next ch-5 sp, (sc in 2nd ch of next ch-3 sp, ch 3) 14 times; repeat from * across] to next corner ch-5 sp, (sc, ch 5, sc) in 3rd ch of ch-5 sp; repeat from ◊ 2 more times; repeat between [ ], join with sl st in first sc.

Rnd 2: Sl st in each of next 3 chs, ch 1, (sc, ch 5, sc) in same ch, *[ch 3, (sc in 2nd ch of next ch-3 sp, ch 3) across to next corner ch-5 sp], (sc, ch 5, sc) in 3rd ch of next ch-5 sp; repeat from * 2 more times; repeat between [ ], join, fasten off.✣

ASSEMBLY DIAGRAM

First Row First Block	First Row Second Block
Second Row First Block	Second Row Second Block

"To see a World in a Grain of Sand,
And a Heaven in a Wild Flower,
Hold Infinity in the palm of your hand,
And Eternity in an hour. . . ."

—WILLIAM BLAKE

Antique Poppies

Designer: Dorris Brooks

Size: 43½" x 69".

Materials: Worsted-weight yarn — 17 oz. each red, green and gold, 8½ oz. lt. yellow; tapestry needle; H crochet hook or size needed to obtain gauge.

Gauge: Rnds 1-5 of Large Motif = 4½". Large Motif is 8½" across. Small Motif is 3½" square.

Skill Level: ★★★ Advanced

INSTRUCTIONS

LARGE MOTIF (make 40)

NOTES: For **beginning popcorn (beg pc),** ch 3, 3 dc in ring, drop lp from hook, insert hook in top of ch-3, pick up dropped lp, draw through st.

For **popcorn (pc),** 4 dc in ring, drop lp from hook, insert hook in first st of 4-dc group, pick up dropped lp, draw through st.

Do not join rnds unless otherwise stated. Mark first st of each rnd.

Rnd 1: With red, ch 4, sl st in first ch to form ring, beg pc, ch 3, (pc, ch 3) 3 times (4 ch-3 sps).

Rnd 2: For **petals,** (sc, 4 dc, sc) in each ch sp around (4 petals).

Rnd 3: Working behind petals, in ch sps on rnd 1, ch 4, sc in sp between center 2 dc on first petal, ch 4, *sc around back bar (see illustration) of next sc, ch 4, sc in sp between center 2 dc on next petal, ch 4; repeat from * 2 more times (8 ch-4 sps).

BACK BAR OF SC

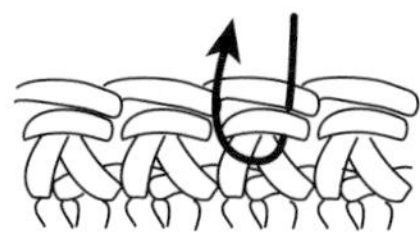

Rnd 4: (Sc, 5 dc, sc) in each ch sp around, join with sl st in first sc.

Rnd 5: Ch 1, sc in each st around, join, fasten off.

Rnd 6: Join green with sc around back bar of sc between any 2 petals, (*ch 7, sc in 2nd ch from hook, hdc in each of next 2 chs, dc in each of next 3 chs*, sc around back bar of sc between next 2 petals) 7 times; repeat between **, join (8 leaves).

Rnd 7: Ch 1, skip first sc; *[working on opposite side of chs on leaf, skip first ch, sc in next 5 chs, 3 sc in next st, sc in next 5 sts], skip next st; repeat from * 6 more times; repeat between [ ], join, fasten off (104 sc).

Rnd 8: Join gold with sc in center sc of any 3-sc group, 2 sc in same st, ◊[hdc in each of next 2 sts, dc in next st, skip next 2 sts; to **tr next 2 sts tog,** *yo 2 times, insert hook in next st, yo, draw lp through, (yo, draw through 2 lps on hook) 2 times; repeat from *, yo, draw through all 3 lps on hook; skip next 2 sts, dc in next st, hdc in each of next 2 sts], 3 sc in next st; repeat from ◊ 6 more times; repeat between [ ], join (80 sts).

Rnd 9: Ch 1, sc in each of first 3 sts, (*hdc in each of next 2 sts, dc in each of next 3 sts, hdc in each of next 2 sts*, sc in each of next 3 sts) 7 times; repeat between **, join, fasten off.

Rnd 10: Join lt. yellow with sl st in 2nd st, ch 2, 2 hdc in same st, hdc in next 9 sts, (3 hdc in next st, hdc in next 9 sts) around, join with sl st in top of ch-2, fasten off (96 hdc).

With lt. yellow, sew Large Motifs together through **back lps** according to Assembly Diagram on page 130.

SMALL MOTIF (make 28)

Rnd 1: With red, ch 4, sl st in first ch to form ring, beg pc, ch 3, (pc, ch 3) 3 times, join with sl st in beg pc (4 ch-3 sps).

Rnd 2: Join green with sl st in any ch sp, ch 3, (2 dc, ch 1, 3 dc) in same sp, ch 1, *(3 dc, ch 1, 3 dc) in next ch sp, ch 1; repeat from * around, join with sl st in top of ch-3, fasten off (24 dc, 8 ch-1 sps).

Rnd 3: Join lt. yellow with sl st in first ch sp, ch 3, (2 dc, ch 1, 3 dc) in same sp, 3 dc in next ch sp, *(3 dc, ch 1, 3 dc) in next ch sp, 3 dc in next ch sp; repeat from * around, join, fasten off (36 dc, 4 ch-1 sps).

Matching sts, with lt. yellow, sew Small Motifs through **back lps** to sps between Large Motifs as

Continued on page 130

Iris Splendor

Designer: Cathy C. Ruby

Size: 50" x 55½".

Materials: Worsted-weight yarn — 43 oz. off-white, 3 oz. each purple, dk. brown, lt. gold and dk. green; I afghan hook and I crochet hook or size needed to obtain gauge.

Gauge: 3 afghan sts = 1"; 3 afghan st rows = 1".

Skill Level: ★★ Average

INSTRUCTIONS

AFGHAN

Row 1: With afghan hook and off-white, ch 135; leaving all lps on hook, insert hook in 2nd ch from hook, yo, draw lp through, (insert hook in next ch, yo, draw lp through) across, **do not** turn; to **work lps off hook,** yo, draw through one lp on hook (see ill. a), (yo, draw through 2 lps on hook) across leaving one lp on hook at end of row (see ill. b), **do not** turn (135 sts).

NOTES: Always skip first vertical bar at beginning of each row. Lp remaining on hook at end of each row is first st of next row.

For **afghan st,** insert hook under next vertical bar (see ill. c), yo, draw lp through; for **last st,** insert hook under last bar and st directly behind it (see ill. d), yo, draw lp through.

For **purl st (purl),** holding yarn to front, insert hook from right to left under next vertical bar, yo, draw lp through.

For **cross st,** skip next vertical bar, insert hook under next vertical bar, yo, draw lp through, insert hook under skipped vertical bar, yo, draw lp through.

Row 2: Afghan st 27, *(cross st, purl 1) 9 times, afghan st 27; repeat from *; work sts off hook.

Row 3: Afghan st 27, *(purl 2, afghan st 1) 9 times, afghan st 27; repeat from *; work sts off hook.

Rows 4-50: Repeat rows 2 and 3 alternately, ending with row 2.

Row 51: (Cross st, purl 1) 9 times, *afghan st 27, (cross st, purl 1) 9 times; repeat from *; work sts off hook.

Row 52: (Purl 2, afghan st 1) 9 times, *afghan st 27, (purl 2, afghan st 1) 9 times; repeat from *; work sts off hook.

Rows 53-100: Repeat rows 51 and 52 alternately.

Rows 101-150: Repeat rows 2 and 3 alternately. At end of last row, **do not** fasten off.

BORDER

Rnd 1: Working around outer edge, with crochet hook, 2 sc in first st, *sc in each st across to last st, (2 sc, ch 2, 2 sc) in last st; working in ends of rows, skip first row, sc in next 148 rows, skip last row*; working in starting ch on opposite side of row 1, (2 sc, ch 2, 2 sc) in first st; repeat between **, 2 sc in same st as first st; to **join,** hdc in first sc (139 sc on each short end between corner ch-2 sps, 152 sc on each long edge between corner ch-2 sps).

Rnd 2: Ch 1, (sc, ch 1, sc) around joining hdc, sc in each st around with (sc, ch 1, sc) in each cor-

AFGHAN STITCH

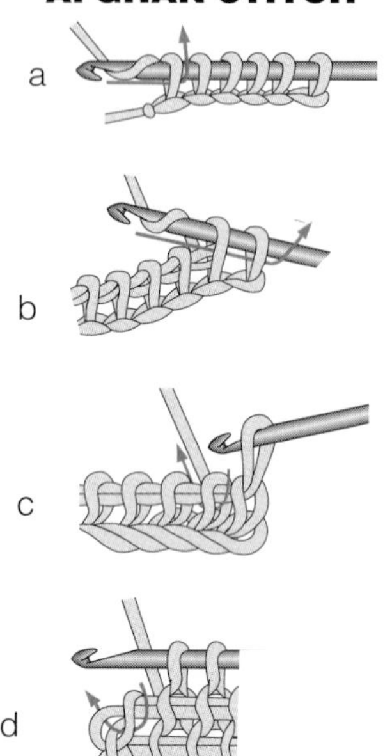

Continued on page 131

Lavender Bouquet

Designer: Carol Alexander

for Monsanto's Designs for America Program

Size: 50½" x 62".

Materials: Worsted-weight yarn — 27 oz. purple, 18 oz. burgundy, 3 oz. lt. green; tapestry needle; G crochet hook or size needed to obtain gauge.

Gauge: 6 sts = 2"; rows 1-3 = 1". Rnd 1 = 2" across; Motif = 5" square. Strip B = 5¼" wide.

Skill Level: ★★ Average

INSTRUCTIONS

MOTIF (make 44)

Rnd 1: With Burgundy, ch 4, sl st in first ch to form ring, ch 1, (sc, ch 3, tr, ch 3) 4 times in ring, join with sl st in first sc, fasten off (8 sts).

Rnd 2: Skipping ch sps, join purple with sl st in first sc, ch 8, sc in next tr, ch 5, (tr in next sc, ch 5, sc in next tr, ch 5) around, join with sl st in 3rd ch of ch-8, fasten off (8 ch sps, 4 tr, 4 sc).

Rnd 3: Join lt. green with sl st in any tr, ch 3, 2 dc in same st, sc in next ch sp, (2 tr, ch 1, 2 tr) in next sc, sc in next ch sp, *3 dc in next tr, sc in next ch sp, (2 tr, ch 1, 2 tr) in next sc, sc in next ch sp; repeat from * around, join with sl st in top of ch-3, fasten off (36 sts).

Rnd 4: Join purple with sc in any ch-1 sp, 2 sc in same sp, (*skip next st, sc in next st, 2 sc in each of next 2 sts, sc in each of next 2 sts, 2 sc in each of next 2 sts, sc in next st*, 3 sc in next ch-1 sp) 3 times; repeat between **, join with sl st in first sc, fasten off (60).

Rnd 5: Join burgundy with sc in center st of any 3-sc group, ch 1, sc in same st, [◊skip next 2 sts, (hdc, ch 1, hdc) in next st, skip next 2 sts, *(dc, ch 1, dc) in next st, skip next 2 sts; repeat from * (hdc, ch 1, hdc) in next st, skip next 2 sts◊, (sc, ch 1, sc) in center st of next 3-sc group]; repeat between [ ] 2 more times; repeat between ◊◊, join with sl st in first sc.

Rnd 6: Sl st in next ch sp, ch 1, 2 sc in same sp; *[working in sp between 2-st groups, sc in next sp, 3 hdc in next sp, (2 dc, ch 2, 2 dc) in next sp, 3 hdc in next sp, sc in next sp], 2 sc in next ch-1 sp; repeat from * 2 more times; repeat between [ ], join.

Rnd 7: Ch 1, sc in each of first 3 sts, *[hdc in each of next 3 sts, dc in each of next 2 sts, (2 dc, ch 2, 2 dc) in next ch sp, skip next st, dc in next st, hdc in each of next 3 sts], sc in next 5 sts; repeat from * 2 more times; repeat between [ ], sc in each of last 2 sts, join, fasten off (17 sts on each edge between corner ch sps.

Matching sts, sew 11 Motifs end to end forming a strip. Repeat with remaining Motifs making a total of four strips of 11 Motifs each.

Edging

Working on long edge of one strip in **front lps** only, join burgundy with sl st in corner ch sp, skip next st, (sc in next st, 3 dc in next st, skip next 2 sts) across, sl st in next corner ch sp. Repeat on opposite side of strip.

Work edging on long edges of each strip.

PANEL (make 5)

Row 1: With purple, ch 29, sc in 2nd ch from hook, skip next 2 chs, *(sc, ch 1, dc) in next ch, skip next 2 chs; repeat from * across to last ch, sc in last ch, turn (18 sts, 8 ch sps).

Rows 2-172: Ch 1, sc in first st, (sc, ch 1, dc) in each ch sp across to last st, sc in last st, turn. At end of last row, fasten off.

Alternating Panels and strips, sew long edge of Panels to **back lps** of rnd 7 on strips below Edging.

BORDER

Join burgundy with sc in top right-hand corner st, 5 dc in same st, [◊*skip next 2 sts, (sc, 3 dc) in next st; repeat from * around to one or two sts before next corner st◊, (sc, 5 dc) in next corner st]; repeat between [ ] 2 more times; repeat between ◊◊, join with sl st in first sc, fasten off. Tack Edging on long edges of strips down as desired.✣

Nature's Palette

Designer: Katherine Eng

Size: 45" x 61".

Materials: Worsted-weight yarn — 20 oz. navy, 11 oz. each royal blue and green, 6 oz. each lt. purple, med. purple and lt. blue; tapestry needle; F and H crochet hooks or size needed to obtain gauge.

Gauge: H hook, Rnd 1 of Motif = 1¾". Each Motif is 4" square.

Skill Level: ★★ Average

Note: Use H hook unless otherwise stated.

INSTRUCTIONS

MOTIF A (make 59)

Rnd 1: With royal blue, ch 4, sl st in first ch to form ring, ch 3, 2 dc in ring, ch 2, (3 dc in ring, ch 2) 3 times, join with sl st in top of ch-3, fasten off (12 dc, 4 ch-2 sps).

Rnd 2: Join lt. purple with sl st in any ch sp, ch 3, (2 dc, ch 2, 3 dc) in same sp, ch 2, *(3 dc, ch 2, 3 dc) in next ch sp, ch 2; repeat from * around, join, fasten off (24 dc, 8 ch-2 sps).

Rnd 3: Join green with sc in any corner ch sp, ch 2, sc in same sp, *[ch 1, skip next st, sc in next st, ch 1, skip next st; working over next ch sp, (hdc, ch 1, hdc) in center dc of 3-dc group on rnd before last, ch 1, skip next st on last rnd, sc in next st, ch 1, skip next st], (sc, ch 2, sc) in next ch sp; repeat from * 2 more times; repeat between [ ], join with sl st in first sc, fasten off (24 sts, 20 ch-1 sps, 4 ch-2 sps).

Rnd 4: Join navy with sc in any corner ch-2 sp, ch 3, sc in same sp, sc in each st and in each ch-1 sp around with (sc, ch 3, sc) in each corner ch-2 sp, join, fasten off (13 sts on each side between corner ch-3 sps).

MOTIF B (make 58)

Rnd 1: With lt. blue, repeat same rnd of Motif A.

Rnd 2: With med. purple, repeat same rnd of Motif A.

Rnds 3-4: Repeat same rnds of Motif A.

Matching sts, with navy, starting with Motif A in any corner, sew Motifs together alternately through **back lps** in 9 rows of 13 Motifs each.

BORDER

Rnd 1: Working around outer edge, join navy with sc in any corner ch-3 sp, ch 3, sc in same sp, sc in each st, in ch-3 sps on each side of seams and hdc in each seam around with (sc, ch 3, sc) in each corner ch-3 sp, join with sl st in first sc, **turn** (143 sc on each short end between corner ch-3 sps, 207 sc on each long edge between corner ch-3 sps).

Rnd 2: Sl st in next st, ch 1, sc in same st, *ch 1, skip next st, (sc in next st, ch 1, skip next st) across to next corner ch sp, (sc, ch 3, sc) in next ch sp; repeat from * around, ch 1, skip last st, join, **turn,** fasten off.

Rnd 3: Join green with sl st in any corner ch-3 sp, ch 4, hdc in same sp, *[ch 1, hdc in next st, ch 1, skip next ch-1 sp, (hdc in next st, ch 1, skip next ch-1 sp) across to st before next corner ch-3 sp, hdc in next st, ch 1], (hdc, ch 2, hdc) in next corner ch-3 sp; repeat from * 2 more times; repeat between [ ], join with sl st in 2nd ch of ch-4, **turn.**

Rnd 4: Sl st in next ch-1 sp, ch 1, sc in same sp, *ch 1, skip next st, (sc in next ch-1 sp, ch 1, skip next st) across to next corner ch-2 sp, (sc, ch 3, sc) in next corner ch-2 sp; repeat from * around, ch 1, skip last st, join with sl st in first sc, **turn,** fasten off.

Rnds 5-6: With navy, repeat rnds 3 and 4. At end of last rnd, **do not** fasten off.

Rnd 7: Ch 3, dc in each st and in each ch-1 sp around with (2 dc, ch 2, 2 dc) in each corner ch-2 sp, join with sl st in top of ch-3, **do not** turn, fasten off (161 dc on each short end between corner ch-2 sps, 225 dc on each long edge between corner ch-2 sps).

Rnd 8: Join lt. blue with sl st in first corner ch-2 sp before one short end, ch 3, (2 dc, ch 2, 3 dc) in same sp, [skip next 2 sts, sc in next st, skip next 2 sts, *(3 dc, ch 2, 3 dc) in next st, skip next 2 sts, sc in next st, skip next 2 sts; repeat from * across

Continued on page 132

Secret Garden

Designer: Sandra Miller Maxfield

Size: 50" x 61" not including Fringe.

Materials: Worsted-weight yarn — 43 oz. blue/green/rose variegated, 9 oz. each rose, lt. pink, green and off-white; tapestry needle; I crochet hook or size needed to obtain gauge.

Gauge: 3 dc = 1"; two 3-dc groups = 1½"; two 3-dc group rnds worked in pattern = 1¼". Motif is 4½" square.

Skill Level: ★★ Average

INSTRUCTIONS

CENTER MOTIFS

First Motif

Rnd 1: With rose, ch 2, 6 sc in 2nd ch from hook, **do not** join (6 sc).

Rnd 2: 2 sc in each st around, join with sl st in first sc, fasten off (12).

Rnd 3: Join lt. pink with sc in any st, (ch 2, dc, ch 2, sc) in same st, skip next st, *(sc, ch 2, dc, ch 2, sc) in next st, skip next st; repeat from * around, join (6 petals).

Rnd 4: Working behind petals, ch 1, (sc around post of next dc, ch 3) around, join (6 ch-3 sps).

Rnd 5: Sl st in first ch sp, ch 1, (sc, ch 2, dc, tr, dc, ch 2, sc) in same sp and in each ch sp around, join, fasten off.

Rnd 6: Working behind petals, join rose with sc around post of any dc, ch 2, (sc around post of next dc, ch 2) around, join, fasten off (12 ch-2 sps).

Rnd 7: Join green with sc in any ch sp, 2 sc in same sp, 3 sc in next ch sp, (3 dc, ch 2, 3 dc) in next ch sp, *3 sc in each of next 2 ch sps, (3 dc, ch 2, 3 dc) in next ch sp; repeat from * around, join, fasten off (8 3-sc groups, 8 3-dc groups, 4 ch-2 sps).

Rnd 8: Join off-white with sl st in any corner ch sp, ch 3, (2 dc, ch 2, 3 dc) in same sp, *[3 dc in sp between next 3-dc group and next 3-sc group, 3 dc in sp between last 3-sc group and next 3-sc group, 3 dc in sp between last 3-sc group and next 3-dc group], (3 dc, ch 2, 3 dc) in next corner ch sp; repeat from * 2 more times; repeat between [ ], join with sl st in top of ch-3, fasten off (20 3-dc groups, 4 ch-2 sps).

Next Motif (make 2)

Rnds 1-7: Repeat same rnds of First Motif.

Rnd 8: Join off-white with sl st in any corner ch sp, ch 3, (2 dc, ch 2, 3 dc) in same sp, *[3 dc in sp between next 3-dc group and next 3-sc group, 3 dc in sp between last 3-sc group and next 3-sc group, 3 dc in sp between last 3-sc group and next 3-dc group], (3 dc, ch 2, 3 dc) in next corner ch sp; repeat from *; repeat between [ ], 3 dc in next corner ch sp, ch 1, sl st in corner ch sp of last Motif made as shown in Assembly Diagram on page 132, ch 1, 3 dc in same sp on this Motif; repeat between [ ], join with sl st in top of ch-3, fasten off.

CORNER MOTIF (make 6)

Work same as Center Motif First Motif.

Matching sts and corner ch sps, with off-white, sew three Motifs together through **back lps** as shown in diagram. Repeat with remaining Motifs for other corner.

AFGHAN

NOTE: For shell, (3 dc, ch 2, 3 dc) in next st or ch sp.

Rnd 1: Working around outer edge of Center Motifs, join variegated with sl st in end ch sp as shown in diagram, ch 3, (2 dc, ch 2, 3 dc) in same sp, [*(3 dc in next sp between 3-dc groups) 4 times, shell in next ch sp, (3 dc in next sp between 3-dc groups) 4 times*, ◊ch 1, skip next 2 joined ch sps; repeat between **; repeat from ◊ one more time], shell in next ch sp; repeat between [ ], join with sl st in top of ch-3 (64 3-dc groups, 8 ch-2 sps, 4 ch-1 sps).

Rnds 2-12: Sl st in each of next 2 sts, sl st in next ch sp, (ch 3, 2 dc, ch 2, 3 dc) in same sp, 3 dc in each sp between 3-dc groups and shell in each shell around with (ch 1, skip next ch-1) at

Continued on page 132

Spring Meadows

Designer: Jennifer Christiansen McClain

Size: 46" x 59".

Materials: Worsted-weight yarn — 25 oz. off-white, 12 oz. each dk. green, med. blue and purple, 8½ oz. each lt. green, lt. blue and lavender; H crochet hook or size needed to obtain gauge.

Gauge: Rnds 1-2 of Motif = 3½". Each Motif is 6¼" square.

Skill Level: ★★ Average

INSTRUCTIONS

MOTIF A (make 21)

Rnd 1: With med. blue, ch 4, sl st in first ch to form ring, ch 1, sc in ring, ch 5, sc in ring, ch 9, (sc, ch 5, sc, ch 9) 3 times in ring, join with sl st in first sc (8 sc, 4 ch-9 lps, 4 ch-5 lps).

Rnd 2: Working behind ch lps, ch 3, (sl st in next sc, ch 3) 7 times, join with sl st in joining sl st on last rnd, fasten off (8 ch-3 sps).

Rnd 3: Join off-white with sc in 5th ch of any ch-9 lp on rnd 1, ch 2, sc in same ch; *[working behind next ch-5 lp on rnd 1, 3 dc in next ch-3 sp on rnd 2, (sc, ch 2, sc) in 3rd ch of next ch-5 lp on rnd 1, 3 dc in same ch-3 sp on rnd 2 as last 3 dc], (sc, ch 2, sc) in 5th ch of next ch-9 lp on rnd 1; repeat from * 2 more times; repeat between [ ], join with sl st in first sc, fasten off (24 dc, 16 sc, 8 ch-2 sps).

Rnd 4: Join lt. blue with sc in center dc of first 3-dc group, *[ch 4, skip next ch-2 sp, sc in center dc of next 3-dc group, dc in next corner ch-2 sp, (ch 1, dc) 5 times in same sp], sc in center dc of next 3-dc group; repeat from * 2 more times; repeat between [ ], join, fasten off (20 ch-1 sps, 4 ch-4 sps).

Rnd 5: Join med. blue with sc in center ch-1 sp on any corner, ch 2, sc in same sp, *[ch 1, sc in next ch-1 sp, ch 1, hdc in next ch-1 sp, ch 1; working over ch-4 sp on last rnd, (dc, ch 1, dc, ch 1, dc) in next ch-2 sp on rnd 3, ch 1, hdc in next ch-1 sp, ch 1, sc in next ch-1 sp, ch 1], (sc, ch 2, sc) in next corner ch-1 sp; repeat from * 2 more times; repeat between [ ], join, fasten off (36 sts, 32 ch-1 sps, 4 ch-2 sps).

Rnd 6: Join off-white with sc in any corner ch-2 sp, ch 2, sc in same sp, *[ch 1, (sc in next ch-1 sp, ch 1) across] to next corner ch-2 sp, (sc, ch 2, sc) in next ch-2 sp; repeat from * 2 more times; repeat between [ ], join (40 sc, 36 ch-1 sps, 4 ch-2 sps).

Rnd 7: Ch 1, sc in each st and in each ch-1 sp around with (sc, ch 2, sc) in each corner ch-2 sp, join, fasten off (21 sc on each edge between corner ch-2 sps).

MOTIF B (make 21)

Using purple instead of med. blue and lavender instead of lt. blue, work same as Motif A.

MOTIF C (make 21)

Using dk. green instead of med. blue and lt. green instead of lt. blue, work same as Motif A.

ASSEMBLY

Arrange Motifs according to Assembly Diagram on page 133.

For **first row,** holding first two Motifs right sides together, matching sts and ch sps, join off-white with sc in first corner ch sp, sc in each st across to next ch sp, sc in next corner ch sp, *ch 1; holding next two Motifs together, sc in first corner ch sp, sc in each st across to next corner ch sp, sc in next corner ch sp; repeat from * with remaining Motifs in row, fasten off.

Repeat with remaining Motifs until all Motifs are joined vertically.

Working horizontally across Motifs, join in same manner.

BORDER

Rnd 1: Working around outer edge, join off-white with sc in any corner ch sp, ch 2, sc in same sp, sc in each st, hdc in ch sps on each side of seams and dc in each seam around with (sc, ch 2, sc) in each corner ch sp, join with sl st in first sc (167 sc on each short end between corner ch-2 sps, 215 sc on each long edge between corner ch-2 sps).

Continued on page 133

Wisteria Wonder

Designer: Katherine Eng

Size: 42½" x 61".

Materials: Worsted-weight yarn — 14 oz. each raspberry and med. purple, 11 oz. each royal blue and lt. blue, 7 oz. lt. purple; tapestry needle; G crochet hook or size needed to obtain gauge.

Gauge: Rnds 1-2 of Motif = 2¼". Each Motif is 6¼" square.

Skill Level: ★★ Average

INSTRUCTIONS

MOTIF (54)

Rnd 1: With raspberry, ch 4, sl st in first ch form ring, ch 1, 8 sc in ring, join with sl st in first sc (8 sc).

NOTES: For **beginning cluster (beg cl),** ch 3, (yo, insert hook in same st, yo, draw lp through, yo, draw through 2 lps on hook) 2 times, yo, draw through all 3 lps on hook.

For **cluster (cl),** yo, insert hook in next st, yo, draw lp through, yo, draw through 2 lps on hook, (yo, insert hook in same st, yo, draw lp through, yo, draw through 2 lps on hook) 2 times, yo, draw through all 4 lps on hook.

Rnd 2: Beg cl, ch 2, (cl, ch 2) around, join with sl st in top of beg cl, fasten off (8 ch-2 sps).

Rnd 3: Join lt. purple with sc in any ch sp, (sc, ch 2, 2 sc) in same sp, (2 sc, ch 2, 2 sc) in each ch sp around, join with sl st in first sc, fasten off.

Rnd 4: Join med. purple with sc in any ch sp, *[ch 2, (3 dc, ch 2, 3 dc) in next ch sp, ch 2], sc in next ch sp; repeat from * 2 more times; repeat between [ ], join (28 sts, 12 ch-2 sps).

Rnd 5: Ch 1, sc in each st and 2 sc in each ch sp around with (sc, ch 2, sc) in each corner ch sp, join, fasten off (52 sc, 4 ch-2 sps).

Rnd 6: Join lt. blue with sl st in any corner ch sp, ch 3, (dc, ch 2, 2 dc) in same sp, *[sc in next st, (skip next st, 3 dc in next st, skip next st, sc in next st) across] to next corner ch sp, (2 dc, ch 2, 2 dc) in next ch sp; repeat from * 2 more times; repeat between [ ], join with sl st in top of ch-3, fasten off (68 sts, 4 ch-2 sps).

Rnd 7: Join royal blue with sc in any corner ch sp, ch 2, sc in same sp, *[ch 1, sc in next st, ch 1, dc in next sc, ch 1, (sc in center dc of next 3-dc group, ch 1, dc in next sc, ch 1) 3 times, skip next st, sc in next st, ch 1], (sc, ch 2, sc) in next corner ch sp; repeat from * 2 more times; repeat between [ ], join with sl st in first sc, fasten off (44 sts, 40 ch-1 sps, 4 ch-2 sps).

Rnd 8: Join raspberry with sc in any corner ch-2 sp, ch 2, sc in same sp, *[ch 1, (sc in next ch-1 sp, ch 1) across] to next corner ch-2 sp, (sc, ch 2, sc) in next ch-2 sp; repeat from * 2 more times; repeat between [ ], join, fasten off (12 sc and 11 ch-1 sps on each side between corner ch-2 sps).

Matching sts and ch sps, with raspberry, sew Motifs together through **back lps** in 6 rows of 9 Motifs each.

BORDER

Rnd 1: Working around outer edge, join raspberry with sc in any corner ch-2 sp, ch 3, sc in same sp, sc in each st, in each ch-1 sp and in ch-2 sps on each side of seams around with hdc in each seam and (sc, ch 3, sc) in each corner ch-2 sp, join with sl st in first sc, **turn** (155 sc on each short end between corner ch-3 sps, 233 sc on each long edge between corner ch-3 sps).

Rnd 2: Sl st in next st, ch 1, sc in same st, *ch 1, skip next st, (sc in next st, ch 1, skip next st) across to next corner ch sp, (sc, ch 3, sc) in next ch sp; repeat from * 3 more times, ch 1, skip last st, join, **turn, f**asten off.

Rnd 3: Join lt. purple with sc in any corner ch-3 sp, ch 3, sc in same sp, *[sc in next st, (ch 1, skip next ch-1 sp, sc in next st) across] to next corner ch-3 sp, (sc, ch 3, sc) in next ch sp; repeat from * 2 more times; repeat between [ ], join, **do not** turn.

Rnd 4: Ch 1, sc in each st and in each ch-1 sp around with (sc, ch 3, sc) in each corner ch-3 sp, join, fasten off (161 sc on each short end between corner ch-3 sps, 239 sc on each long edge between corner ch-3 sps).

Rnd 5: Join med. purple with sl st in any corner ch-3 sp, ch 3, (2 dc, ch 3, 3 dc) in same sp, ◊[skip next 2 sts, sc in next st, skip next 2 sts, *(2 dc, ch 2, 2 dc) in next st, skip next 2 sts, sc in next st, skip next 2 sts; repeat from * across] to next

Continued on page 133

Antique Poppies

continued from page 117

shown in diagram.

EDGING

Working around outer edge, join lt. yellow with sc in center st of 3-sc group at top right corner (see diagram), 2 sc in same st, *[(sc in next 11 sts, 3 sc in next st, sc in next 8 sts, sc next 2 sts tog, sc in next st, skip next seam, sc in next st, sc next 2 sts tog, sc in next 8 sts, 3 sc in next st) across to last Large Motif on this side], (sc in next 11 sts, 3 sc in next st) 2 times; repeat from * 2 more times; repeat between [ ], sc in next 11 sts, 3 sc in next st, sc in last 11 sts, join with sl st in first sc, fasten off.

TRIANGLE MOTIF

Row 1: Working in indentation between any 2 Large Motifs, join red with sl st in 3rd st on Edging before 2 sts at indentation, skip next 3 sts, (pc, ch 3, pc) in next st, skip next 2 sts, sl st in next st, **do not** turn, fasten off (2 pc, 1 ch-3 sp).

Row 2: Join green with sl st in 3rd st on Edging before joining sl st on last row, skip next 2 sts, dc in same st as joining sl st on last row, (3 dc, ch 1, 3 dc) in next ch sp, dc in same st as last sl st on last row, skip next 2 sts on Edging, sl st in next st, **do not** turn, fasten off (8 dc, 1 ch-1 sp).

Row 3: Join lt. yellow with sl st in 2nd st on Edging before joining sl st on last row, skip next st, 2 dc in sp between next 2 dc, (3 dc, ch 1, 3 dc) in next ch sp, dc in sp between last 2 dc, skip next st on Edging, sl st in next st, fasten off.

Repeat in each indentation around outer edge of afghan.

OUTER EDGING

Working around outer edge, join gold with sc in center sc of 3-sc group at top right corner (see diagram), 2 sc in same st, *[(sc in each st across to 2 sts before next Triangle Motif, sc next 2 sts tog, sc in first st on Triangle Motif, sc next 2 sts tog, sc in each of next 2 sts, 3 sc in next ch sp, sc in each of next 2 sts, sc next 2 sts tog, sc in last st on Triangle Motif, sc next 2 sts tog) across to last Large Motif on this side], (sc in each st across to center st of next 3-sc group, 3 sc in next st) 2 times; repeat from * 2 more times; repeat between [ ], sc in each st across to center st of next 3-sc group, 3 sc in next st, sc in each st across, join with sl st in first sc, fasten off.✥

ASSEMBLY DIAGRAM

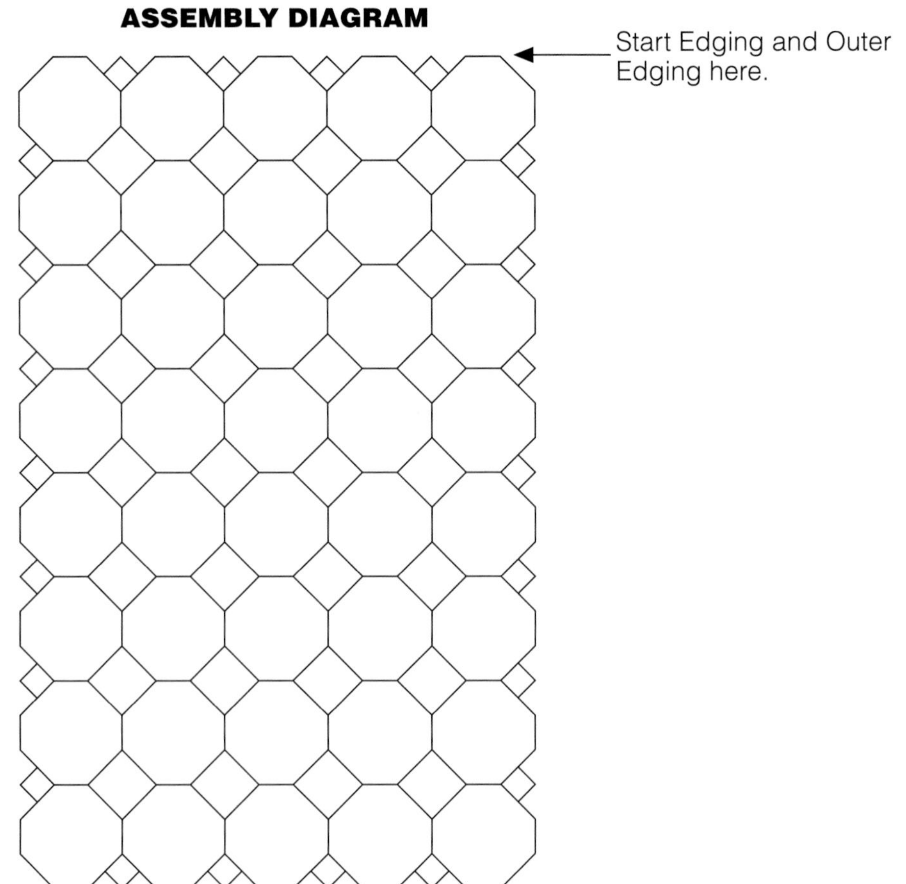

Iris Splender

continued from page 118

ner ch sp, join with sl st in first sc (141 sc on each short end between corner ch-1 sps, 154 sc on each long edge between corner ch-1 sps).

Rnd 3: Sl st in next ch sp, ch 4, dc in same st, *ch 1, skip next st, (dc in next st, ch 1, skip next st) across to next corner ch sp, (dc, ch 1, dc) in next ch sp, ch 1, (dc in next st, ch 1, skip next st) across* to next corner ch sp, (dc, ch 1, dc) in next ch sp; repeat between **, join with sl st in 3rd ch of ch-4 (72 dc and 71 ch-1 sps on each short endbetween corner ch sps, 79 dc and 78 ch-1 sps on each long edge between corner ch sps).

Rnd 4: Sl st in next ch sp, ch 1, (sc, ch 1, sc) in same sp, sc in each st and in each ch-1 sp around with (sc, ch 1, sc) in each corner ch sp, join with sl st in first sc (145 sc on each short end between corner ch-1 sps, 159 sc on each long edge between corner ch-1 sps).

Rnd 5: Sl st in next ch sp, ch 4, (2 tr, ch 3, dc in top of last st made, 3 tr) in same sp, [skip next 4 sts, (dc, ch 4, dc in top of last st made, dc) in next st, skip next 4 sts, *(3 tr, ch 3, dc in top of last st made, 3 tr) in next st, skip next 3 sts, (dc, ch 4, dc in top of last st made, dc) in next st, skip next 3 sts; repeat from * across to next corner ch sp, (3 tr, ch 3, dc in top of last st made, 3 tr) in next ch sp, skip next 3 sts, (dc, ch 4, dc in top of last st made, dc) in next st, skip next 3 sts, ◊(3 tr, ch 3, dc in top of last st made, 3 tr) in next st, skip next 3 sts, (dc, ch 4, dc in top of last st made, dc) in next st, skip next 3 sts; repeat from ◊ across] to next corner, (3 tr, ch 3, dc in top of last st made, 3 tr) in next ch sp; repeat between [ ], join with sl st in top of ch-4, fasten off.

FINISHING

Using colors indicated, cross stitch (see illustration) iris over each plain afghan stitch section on Afghan according to Diagram.✣

CROSS STITCH OVER AFGHAN STITCH ILLUSTRATION

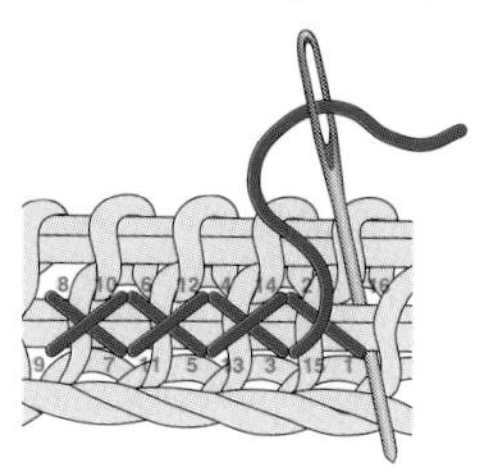

IRIS EMBROIDERY DIAGRAM

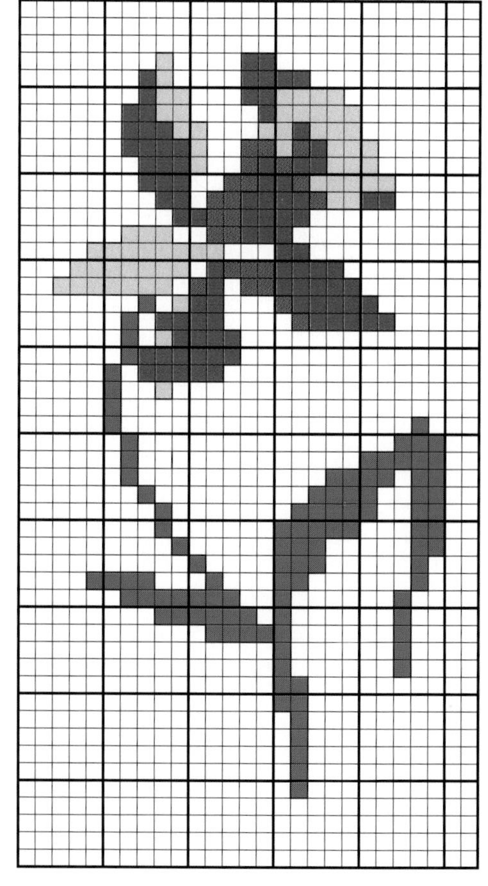

Nature's Palette

continued from page 122

to next corner ch-2 sp, (3 dc, ch 2, 3 dc) in next corner ch-2 sp, skip next st, sc in next st, ◊skip next 2 sts, (3 dc, ch 2, 3 dc) in next st, skip next 2 sts, sc in next st; repeat from ◊ across to one st before next corner ch-2 sp, skip next st], (3 dc, ch 2, 3 dc) in next ch-2 sp; repeat between [ ], join, **turn,** fasten off.

Rnd 9: Join royal blue with sl st in any corner ch sp, ch 3, (2 dc, ch 2, 3 dc) in same sp, ◊[skip next st, sc in next st, skip next st, (2 dc, ch 2, 2 dc) in next sc, *sc in next ch sp, (2 dc, ch 2, 2 dc) in next sc; repeat from * across to 3 sts before next corner ch sp, skip next st, sc in next st, skip next st], (3 dc, ch 2, 3 dc) in next ch sp; repeat from ◊ 2 more times; repeat between [ ], join, sl st in each of next 2 sts, sl st in next corner ch sp, **turn.**

Rnd 10: Ch 3, (2 dc, ch 2, 3 dc) in same sp, ◊[skip next st, sc in next st, skip next st, (2 dc, ch 2, 2 dc) in next sc, *sc in next ch sp, (2 dc, ch 2, 2 dc) in next sc; repeat from * across to 3 sts before next corner ch sp, skip next st, sc in next st, skip next st], (3 dc, ch 2, 3 dc) in next ch sp; repeat from ◊ 2 more times; repeat between [ ], join, **do not** turn.

Rnd 11: With F hook, sl st each of next 2 sts, sl st in next corner ch sp, ch 1, (sc, ch 3, sc, ch 5, sc, ch 3, sc) in same sp, ◊[ch 3, sc in next sc, ch 3, *(sc, ch 3, sc) in next ch sp, ch 3, sc in next sc, ch 3; repeat from * across] to next corner ch sp, (sc, ch 3, sc, ch 5, sc, ch 3, sc) in next ch sp; repeat from ◊ 2 more times; repeat between [ ], join with sl st in first sc, fasten off.✣

Secret Garden

continued from page 125

each indentation, join. At end of last row, fasten off.

Rnd 13: Join off-white with sl st in first ch sp, (ch 3, 2 dc, ch 2, 3 dc) in same sp, 3 dc in each sp between 3-dc groups and shell in each shell around with (ch 1, skip next ch-1) at each indentation, join, fasten off.

Rnds 14-19: Working in color sequence of green, lt. pink, rose, lt. pink, green and off-white, repeat rnd 13.

Matching sts and ch sps, with off-white, sew Corner Motifs to indentations on Afghan through **back lps** only as shown in Assembly Diagram.

Rnd 20: Join variegated with sl st in first ch-2 sp, (ch 3, 2 dc, ch 2, 3 dc) in same sp, 3 dc in each sp between 3-dc groups and in ch sp on each side of seams on Corner Motifs around with shell in each ch-2 sp, join.

Rnds 21-22: Sl st in each of next 2 sts, sl st in next ch sp, (ch 3, 2 dc, ch 2, 3 dc) in same sp, 3 dc in each sp between 3-dc groups around with shell in each shell, join. At end of last rnd, fasten off.

Rnd 23: Join off-white with sl st in first ch sp, (ch 3, 2 dc, ch 2, 3 dc) in same sp, 3 dc in each sp between 3-dc groups around with shell in each shell, join, fasten off.

Rnd 24: With rose, repeat rnd 23.

Rnd 25: With variegated, repeat rnd 23, **do not** fasten off.

Rnds 26-37: Repeat rnd 21. At end of last rnd, fasten off.

BORDER

Row 1: Working across one short end of Afghan, join variegated with sl st in first ch-2 sp, ch 3, dc in same sp, dc in each st across to next ch sp, 2 dc in next ch sp leaving remaining sts unworked, turn.

Rows 2-10: Ch 3, dc in each st across, turn. At end of last row, fasten off.

Repeat on opposite end.

FRINGE

For **each Fringe,** cut 2 strands variegated and one strand rose each 16" long. With all 3 strands held together, fold in half, insert hook in st, draw fold through, draw all loose ends through fold, tighten. Trim ends.

Fringe in every other st on short ends of Afghan.✣

ASSEMBLY DIAGRAM

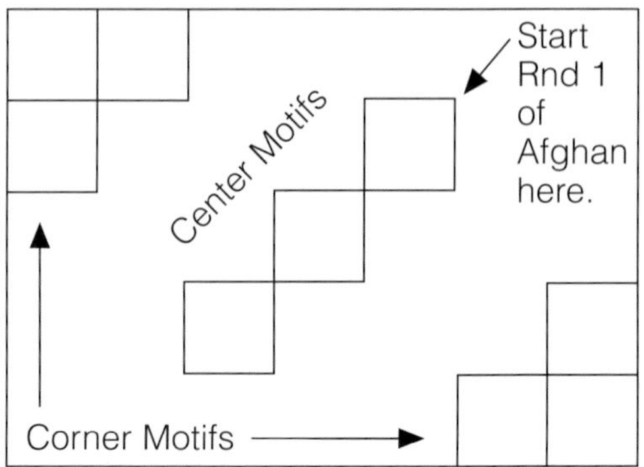

Spring Meadows

continued from page 126

Rnd 2: Sl st in next ch sp, ch 1, (sc, ch 2, sc) in same sp, sc in each st around with (sc, ch 2, sc) in each corner ch sp, join (169 sc on each short end between corner ch-2 sps, 217 sc on each long edge between corner ch-2 sps).

Rnd 3: Sl st in next ch sp, ch 1, (sc, ch 2, sc) in same sp, ◊[skip next st, *(sc, ch 2, sc) in next st, skip next 2 sts; repeat from * across] to next corner ch sp, (sc, ch 2, sc) in next ch sp; repeat from ◊ 2 more times; repeat between [ ], join, fasten off.✣

ASSEMBLY DIAGRAM

C	A	B	C	A	B	C
B	C	A	B	C	A	B
A	B	C	A	B	C	A
C	A	B	C	A	B	C
B	C	A	B	C	A	B
A	B	C	A	B	C	A
C	A	B	C	A	B	C
B	C	A	B	C	A	B
A	B	C	A	B	C	A

A = Motif A
B = Motif B
C = Motif C

Wisteria Wonder

continued from page 129

corner ch-3 sp, (3 dc, ch 3, 3 dc) in next ch sp; repeat from ◊ 2 more times; repeat between [ ], join with sl st in top of ch-3, **turn.**

Rnd 6: Sl st in next sc, ch 1, (sc, ch 2, sc) in same sc, ◊[*ch 2, (sc, ch 2, sc) in next ch-2 sp, ch 2, (sc, ch 2, sc) in next sc; repeat from * across to 3 dc before next corner ch-3 sp, ch 1, skip next dc, (sc, ch 2, sc) in next dc, ch 1, skip next dc, (sc, ch 3, sc) in next corner ch-3 sp, ch 1, skip next dc, ch 1, (sc, ch 2, sc) in next dc, ch 1, skip next dc], (sc, ch 2, sc) in next sc; repeat from ◊ 2 more times; repeat between [ ], join with sl st in first sc, **turn.**

Rnd 7: Join lt. blue with sl st in any corner ch-3 sp, ch 3, (2 dc, ch 3, 3 dc) in same sp, ◊[sc in next ch-2 sp, *(2 dc, ch 2, 2 dc) in next ch-2 sp, sc in next ch-2 sp; repeat from * across] to next corner ch-3 sp, (3 dc, ch 3, 3 dc) in next ch sp; repeat from ◊ 2 more times; repeat between [ ], join with sl st in top of ch-3, **do not** turn, fasten off.

Rnd 8: Join royal blue with sc in any corner ch-3 sp, (ch 3, sc, ch 5, sc, ch 3, sc) in same sp, ◊[ch 1, skip next dc, (sc, ch 3, sc) in next dc, ch 1, skip next dc, sc in next sc, *ch 3, (sc, ch 3, sc) in next ch-2 sp, ch 3, sc in next sc; repeat from * across to 3 dc before next corner ch-3 sp, ch 1, skip next dc, (sc, ch 3, sc) in next dc, ch 1, skip next dc], (sc, ch 3, sc, ch 5, sc, ch 3, sc) in next corner ch-3 sp; repeat from ◊ 2 more times; repeat between [ ], join, fasten off.✣

My Garden

"...As I listened from a beach-chair in the shade
To all the noises that my garden made,
It seemed to me only proper that words
Should be withheld from vegetables and birds. ..."

—W. H. Auden

Peacock Petals

Designer: Maggie Weldon

for Monsanto's Designs for America Program

Size: 56" x 71".

Materials: Worsted-weight yarn — 36 oz. off-white, 27 oz. variegated gold, purple, pink, blue and green; tapestry needle; J crochet hook or size needed to obtain gauge.

Gauge: 2 shells and 1 sc = 2"; rnds 1 and 2 = 2¼" wide. Strip is 7" wide.

Skill Level: ★ Easy

INSTRUCTIONS

STRIP (make 8)

Rnd 1: With off-white, ch 170, sc in 2nd ch from hook, (ch 1, sc in same ch) 2 times, (ch 2, skip next 2 chs, sc in next ch) across to last 3 chs, ch 2, skip next 2 chs, (sc, ch 1, sc, ch 1, sc) in last ch; working on opposite side of ch, (ch 2, skip next 2 chs, sc in next ch) across to last 2 chs, ch 2, skip last 2 chs, join with sl st in first sc, fasten off (118 sc, 118 ch sps).

NOTE: For **shell,** 4 dc in next st or ch sp.

Rnd 2: Join variegated with sl st in first sc, ch 3, 3 dc in same st, sc in next ch sp, shell in next st, (sc in next sp, shell in next st) around, join with sl st in top of ch-3, fasten off (118 shells, 118 sc).

Rnd 3: Join off-white with sc in 3rd dc of first shell, *(ch 4, dc in next sc, ch 4, sc in 3rd dc of next shell) 2 times*, (ch 4, skip next sc, sc in 3rd dc of next shell) 56 times; repeat between **, (ch 4, skip next sc, sc in 3rd dc of next shell) 55 times, ch 4, join with sl st in first sc (120 ch sps).

Rnd 4: Sl st in next ch sp, ch 4, 4 dc in same sp, 5 dc in each of next 3 ch sps, 3 dc in each of next 56 ch sps, 5 dc in each of next 4 ch sps, 3 dc in each of last 56 ch sps, join with sl st in top of ch-3 (8 5-dc groups, 112 3-dc groups).

Rnd 5: Join variegated with sc in first st, ch 1, skip next st, (sc in next st, ch 1, skip next st) around, join with sl st in first sc, fasten off.

Rnd 6: Join off-white with sl st in first ch sp, ch 2, 2 hdc in same sp, 3 hdc in each of next 9 ch sps, 2 hdc in each of next 84 ch sps, 3 hdc in each of next 10 ch sps, 2 hdc in each of last 84 ch sps, join with sl st in top of ch-2, fasten off.

To **join Strips,** skipping all 3-hdc groups on each end, sew long edge of Strips together through **back lps** only.✣

Autumn Bounty

Designer: Sue Childress

Size: 43" x 55".

Materials: Fuzzy worsted-weight yarn — 20 oz. variegated main color (MC) and 4 oz. contrasting color (CC); I crochet hook or size needed to obtain gauge.

Gauge: 3 sts = 1"; rnd 1 = 2¼" across. Each Block is 12" square.

Skill Level: ★★ Average

INSTRUCTIONS

BLOCK (make 12)

Rnd 1: With MC, ch 8, sl st in first ch to form ring, ch 3, 15 dc in ring, join with sl st in top of ch-3 (16 dc).

NOTE: For **cluster (cl),** *yo, insert hook in st, yo, draw lp through, yo, draw through 2 lps on hook; repeat from * 5 more times in same st, yo, draw through all 7 lps on hook.

Rnd 2: Ch 4, cl in next st, ch 1, (dc in next st, ch 1, cl in next st, ch 1) around, join with sl st in 3rd ch of ch-4 (16 ch-1 sps).

Rnd 3: Sl st in first ch-1 sp, ch 3, 6 dc in same sp, ch 1, skip next ch-1 sp, 5 dc in next ch-1 sp, ch 1, skip next ch-1 sp, *7 dc in next ch-1 sp, ch 1, skip next ch-1 sp, 5 dc in next ch-1 sp, ch 1, skip next ch-1 sp; repeat from * around, join with sl st in top of ch-3 (48 dc).

NOTE: For **shell,** (2 dc, ch 2, 2 dc) in next st or sp.

Rnd 4: Ch 3, dc in each of next 2 sts, *[shell in next st, dc in each of next 3 sts, skip next 2 sts, 5 dc in next st, skip next 2 sts], dc in each of next 3 sts; repeat from * 2 more times; repeat between [ ], join (44 dc, 4 shells).

Rnd 5: Ch 3, dc in next 4 sts, *[shell in next ch-2 sp, dc in next 5 sts, ch 1, skip next st, (cl in next st, ch 1, skip next st) 2 times], dc in next 5 sts; repeat from * 2 more times; repeat between [ ], join (40 dc, 12 ch-1 sps, 4 shells).

Rnd 6: Ch 3, dc in next 6 sts, *[shell in next ch-2 sp, dc in next 7 sts, ch 1, (cl in next ch-1 sp, ch 1) 3 times], dc in next 7 sts; repeat from * 2 more times; repeat between [ ], join (56 dc, 16 ch-1 sps, 4 shells).

Rnd 7: Ch 3, dc in next 7 sts, *[skip next st, shell in next ch-2 sp, skip next st, dc in next 8 sts, ch 1, (cl in next ch-1 sp, ch 1) 4 times], dc in next 8 sts; repeat from * 2 more times; repeat between [ ], join (64 dc, 20 ch-1 sps, 4 shells).

Rnd 8: Ch 3, dc in next 8 sts, *[skip next st, shell in next ch-2 sp, skip next st, dc in next 9 sts, 3 dc in each of next 5 ch-1 sps], dc in next 9 sts; repeat from * 2 more times; repeat between [ ], join, fasten off (132 dc, 4 shells).

To **form Strip** (make 3), holding two Blocks wrong sides together, matching sts and working through both thicknesses, join MC with sl st in first ch-2 sp, sl st in each st across to next ch-2 sp, sl st in next ch-2 sp leaving remaining sts unworked, fasten off. Repeat two more times with next two Blocks, ending with one Strip four Blocks long.

Join Strips in same manner, ending with three rows of four Blocks each.

BORDER

Rnd 1: Working around outer edge, join CC with sl st in corner ch-2 sp before either short end, ch 3, (2 dc, ch 2, 3 dc) in same sp, ◊[skip next st, dc in next 36 sts, *(ch 1, cl in next ch-2 sp) 2 times, ch 1, skip next st, dc in next 36 sts; repeat from * across to next corner ch-2 sp], (3 dc, ch 2, 3 dc) in next corner ch-2 sp; repeat from ◊ 2 more times; repeat between [ ], join with sl st in top of ch-3 (114 dc and 6 ch-1 sps across each short end, 150 dc and 9 ch-1 sps across each long edge).

Rnd 2: Sl st in each of next 2 sts, sl st in next ch-2 sp, ch 3, (2 dc, ch 2, 3 dc) in same sp, [skip next st, dc in next 19 sts, skip next st, cl in next st, skip next st, dc in next 16 sts, cl in each of next 3 ch-1 sps, *skip next st, dc in next 16 sts, skip next st, cl in next st, skip next st, dc in next 16 sts, cl in each of next 3 ch-1 sps*, skip next st, dc in next 16 sts, skip next st, cl in next st, skip next st, dc in next 19 sts, skip next st (3 dc, ch 2, 3 dc) in next corner ch-2 sp, skip next st, dc in next 19 sts, skip next st, cl in next st, skip next st, dc in next 16 sts, cl in each of next 3 ch-1 sps; repeat beteen ** 2 times, skip next st, dc in next 16 sts, skip next st, cl in next st, skip next st, dc in next

Continued on page 152

Pepper Patch

Designer: Rosalie De Vries

Size: 53½" x 70".

Materials: Worsted-weight yarn — 21 oz. green, 19 oz. burnt orange and 18 oz. tangerine; H crochet hook or size needed to obtain gauge.

Gauge: Rnds 1-3 of Motif = 3½" across. Each Motif is 10½" x 11½".

Skill Level: ★★★ Advanced

INSTRUCTIONS

FIRST ROW

First Motif

Rnd 1: With tangerine, ch 2, 8 sc in 2nd ch from hook, join with sl st in first sc, fasten off (8 sc).

Rnd 2: Join green with sl st in first st, ch 3, 2 dc in same st, 2 dc in next st, (3 dc in next st, 2 dc in next st) around, join with sl st in top of ch-3, fasten off (20 dc).

NOTE: For **petal,** ch 3, 3 dc in side of sc just made.

Rnd 3: Join burnt orange with sc in first st, petal, skip next st, (sc in next st, petal, skip next st) around, join with sl st in first sc, fasten off (10 petals).

Rnd 4: Join tangerine with sl st in top of ch-3 on first petal, ch 3, 4 dc in same ch, *ch 3, sc in top of next petal, ch 3, 5 dc in top of next petal, ch 3, (sc in top of next petal, ch 3) 2 times*, 5 dc in top of next petal; repeat between **, join with sl st in top of ch-3, fasten off (26 sts, 10 ch-3 sps).

Rnd 5: Join green with sl st in first st, ch 3, dc in each st and 3 dc in each ch-3 sp around with 5 dc in center st of each 5-dc group, join, fasten off (72 dc).

Rnd 6: Join burnt orange with sc in 3rd st, petal, skip next st, sc in next st, petal, skip next st, *(sc in next st, petal, skip next 2 sts) 4 times, (sc in next st, petal, skip next st) 2 times, (sc in next st, petal, skip next 2 sts) 2 times, sc in next st, petal, skip next 3 sts, (sc in next st, petal, skip next 2 sts) 2 times*, (sc in next st, petal, skip next st) 2 times; repeat between **, join with sl st in first sc, fasten off (26 petals).

Rnd 7: Join tangerine with sc in top of ch-3 on first petal, *ch 7, (sc in top of next petal, ch 3) 5 times, sc in top of next petal, ch 7, (sc in top of next petal, ch 3) 6 times*, sc in top of next petal; repeat between **, join, **do not** fasten off (26 sc, 22 ch-3 sps, 4 ch-7 lps).

Rnd 8: Ch 1, sc in first st, *9 sc in next ch-7 lp, (sc in next st, 2 sc in next ch-3 sp) 5 times, sc in next st, 9 sc in next ch-7 lp, (sc in next st, 2 sc in next ch-3 sp) 6 times*, sc in next st; repeat between **, join, fasten off (106 sc).

Rnd 9: Join green with sl st in first st, ch 2, hdc in each st around with (sc, ch 4, sc) in 5th st of each 9-sc corner, join with sl st in top of ch-2, fasten off (110 sts, 4 ch-4 sps).

Rnd 10: Join burnt orange with sl st in first st, ch 2, hdc in each st around with (2 sc, hdc, 2 sc) in each ch-4 sp, join, fasten off (130 sts).

Rnd 11: Join tangerine with sc in first st, sc in each st around with 3 sc in center hdc on each corner, join with sl st in first sc, fasten off (138 sc).

NOTE: For picot, ch 4, dc in 4th ch from hook.

Rnd 12: Join green with sl st in center st of first 3-sc group, ch 6, dc in 4th ch from hook, hdc in same st on last rnd, *[picot, skip next 2 sts, (sc in next st, picot, skip next 2 sts) across] to next center corner st, (hdc, picot, hdc) in next corner st; repeat from * 2 more times; repeat between [ ], join with sl st in 2nd ch of ch-6, fasten off (50 picots).

Second Motif

Rnds 1-11: Repeat same rnds of First Motif.

NOTE: For **beginning (beg) joining picot,** inserting hook from back to front, sc in center ch of ch-3 on corner petal of previous Motif, ch 1, dc in 2nd ch of ch-4.

For **joining picot,** ch 2; inserting hook from back to front, sc in center ch of ch-3 on corresponding picot on designated Motif, ch 1, dc in first ch of ch-2.

Rnd 12: Join green with sl st in center st of first 3-sc group; holding this Motif and last Motif made wrong sides together, matching edges, beg joining picot, hdc in same st on last rnd of this Motif, join-

Continued on page 152

Summer Sage

Designer: Anne Halliday

for Monsanto's Designs for America Program

Size: 40" x 60" not including Fringe.

Materials: Worsted-weight yarn — 15 oz. lt. green, 12 oz. each white and purple, 9 oz. black; tapestry needle; I crochet hook or size needed to obtain gauge.

Gauge: 7 sts = 2"; rows 1-6 =1¾". Strip is 3½" wide.

Skill Level: ★★ Average

INSTRUCTIONS

STRIP (make 11)

NOTE: When beginning and ending each color, leave 6" end to be incorporated in Fringe later.

Row 1: With lt. green, ch 452, dc in 6th ch from hook, (ch 1, skip next ch, dc in next ch) across, turn, fasten off (225 dc).

Row 2: Join black with sc in first st, (skip next ch sp, sc in next st) across, turn (225 sc).

Row 3: Ch 1, sc in each st across, turn, fasten off.

NOTE: For **cluster (cl),** ch 3, dc in 3rd ch from hook.

Row 4: Join purple with sc in first st, (cl, skip next 2 sts, sc in next st) across, turn, fasten off (75 cls).

Row 5: Join white with sc in first sc, (skip next cl; working in skipped sts on row 3, dc in each of next 2 sts, sc in next sc on last row) across, turn.

Row 6: Ch 1, sc in first st, (ch 1, skip next st, sc in next st) across, fasten off.

Row 7: Working on opposite side of starting ch, join lt. green with sl st in first ch, ch 4, skip next ch, dc in next ch, (ch 1, skip next ch, dc in next ch) across, turn, fasten off.

Rows 8-12: Repeat rows 2-6.

To **join Strips,** holding right side together, matching sts, whipstitch together with white.

BORDER

Working across one long edge of Afghan, join white with sl st in first st, (ch 1, sl st in next ch sp, skip next st) across to last st, ch 1, sl st in last st, fasten off.

Repeat on opposite long edge.

FRINGE

For **each Fringe,** cut 2 strands of color to match row, each 12" long. Holding both strands together, fold in half, insert hook in end of row, draw fold through, draw all loose ends and tails at end of row through fold, tighten. Trim ends.

Work one Fringe in each sc row and two Fringe in each dc row on each short end of Afghan.✣

Strawberry Fantasies

Size: 47" x 62".

Materials: Worsted-weight yarn — 24 oz. white, 16 oz. pink and 14 oz. dusty rose; H crochet hook or size needed to obtain gauge.

Gauge: Rnds 1-2 of Block = 2½" across. Each Block is 15" square.

Skill Level: ★★★ Advanced

Designer: Elizabeth Owens

INSTRUCTIONS

FIRST ROW

First Block

Rnd 1: With white, ch 5, sl st in first ch to form ring, ch 1, 8 sc in ring, join with sl st in first sc (8 sc).

Rnd 2: Ch 3, (2 dc, ch 3, 2 dc) in next st, *dc in next st, (2 dc, ch 3, 2 dc) in next st; repeat from * around, join with sl st in top of ch-3, fasten off (20 dc, 4 ch-3 sps).

NOTES: For **beginning cluster (beg cl),** ch 3, *yo, insert hook in same st, yo, draw lp through, yo, draw through 2 lps on hook; repeat from * one more time, yo, draw through all 3 lps on hook.

For **cluster (cl),** *yo, insert hook in next ch sp or st, yo, draw lp through, yo, draw through 2 lps on hook; repeat from * 2 more times in same ch sp or st, yo, draw through all 4 lps on hook.

For **horizontal cluster (hcl),** ch 3, *yo, insert hook in top of last st made, yo, draw lp through, yo, draw through 2 lps on hook; repeat from * one more time in same st, yo, draw through all 3 lps on hook.

Rnd 3: Join pink with sl st in first st, beg cl, *[hcl, skip next 2 sts, dc in next ch-3 sp, hcl, cl in same ch-3 sp, hcl, dc in same ch-3 sp, hcl, skip next 2 sts], cl in next st; repeat from * 2 more times; repeat between [ ], join with sl st in top of beg cl (16 hcls, 8 cls, 8 dc).

Rnd 4: Beg cl, *[ch 2, skip next hcl, dc in next dc, ch 4, skip next hcl, cl in top of next cl, ch 4, skip next hcl, dc in next dc, ch 2, skip next hcl], cl in top of next cl; repeat from * 2 more times; repeat between [ ], join, fasten off (8 hcls, 8 dc, 8 ch-4 sps, 8 ch-2 sps).

Rnd 5: Join white with sl st in first st, ch 3, 2 dc in next ch-2 sp, *[dc in next dc, 4 dc in next ch-4 sp, (2 dc, ch 3, 2 dc) in top of next cl, 4 dc in next ch-4 sp], (dc in next dc or in next cl, 2 dc in next ch-2 sp) 2 times; repeat from * 2 more times; repeat between [ ], dc in next dc, 2 dc in last ch-2 sp, join with sl st in top of ch-3, fasten off (76 dc, 4 ch-3 sps).

Rnd 6: Join dusty rose with sl st in first st, beg cl, hcl, skip next 2 sts, ◊dc in next st, hcl, skip next 2 sts, cl in next st, hcl, skip next 2 sts◊, *[dc in next st, hcl, cl in next ch-3 sp, hcl], (dc in next st, hcl, skip next 2 sts, cl in next st, hcl, skip next 2 sts) 3 times; repeat from * 2 more times; repeat between [ ]; repeat between ◊◊, dc in next st, hcl, skip next 2 sts, join with sl st in top of beg cl (32 hcls, 16 cls, 16 dc).

Rnd 7: Beg cl, ch 2, skip next hcl, ◊dc in next dc, ch 2, skip next hcl, cl in next cl, ch 2, skip next hcl◊, *[dc in next dc, ch 5, skip next hcl, cl in next cl, ch 5, skip next hcl], (dc in next dc, ch 2, skip next hcl, cl in next cl, ch 2, skip next hcl) 3 times; repeat from * 2 more times; repeat between [ ]; repeat between ◊◊, dc in next dc, ch 2, skip next hcl, join, fasten off (24 ch-2 sps, 16 cls, 16 dc, 8 ch-5 sps).

Rnd 8: Join white with sl st in first st, ch 3, (2 dc in next ch-2 sp, dc in next dc or in next cl) 3 times, *[5 dc in next ch-5 sp, (2 dc, ch 3, 2 dc) in next cl, 5 dc in next ch-5 sp, dc in next dc], (2 dc in next ch-2 sp, dc in next cl or in next dc) 6 times; repeat from * 2 more times; repeat between [ ], 2 dc in next ch-2 sp, (dc in next cl or in next dc, 2 dc in next ch-2 sp) 2 times, join with sl st in top of ch-3 (132 dc, 4 ch-3 sps).

NOTES: For **beginning shell (beg shell),** ch 3, (dc, ch 2, 2 dc) in same st or sp.

For **shell,** (2 dc, ch 2, 2 dc) in next st or ch sp.

Rnd 9: Beg shell, skip next 2 sts, sc in next st, (skip next 2 sts, shell in next st, skip next 2 sts, sc in next st) 2 times, *[skip next st, shell in next corner ch-3 sp, skip next st, sc in next st, skip next 2 sts], shell in next st, skip next 2 sts, sc in next st,

Continued on page 153

Crimson Carnations

Size: 45½" x 62½".

Materials: Worsted-weight yarn — 20 oz. lt. blue, 13 oz. each med. blue and dk. green, 10 oz. med. green, 5 oz. red and 2 oz. lt. gold; tapestry needle; H crochet hook or size needed to obtain gauge.

Gauge: 13 sts = 4"; rnd 1 of Block = 1" across. Each Block is 8½" square.

Skill Level: ★★★ Advanced

Designer: Jennifer Christiansen McClain

INSTRUCTIONS

BLOCK (make 35)

Rnd 1: With lt. gold, ch 4, sl st in first ch to form ring, ch 1, 8 sc in ring, join with sl st in first sc, fasten off (8 sc).

Rnd 2: For **petals,** join red with sl st in first st, ch 2, (hdc, ch 2, sl st) in same st, (sl st, ch 2, hdc, ch 2, sl st) in each st around, join with sl st in first sl st (8 petals).

Rnd 3: Ch 3; (working behind petals, sl st in 2nd sl st between next 2 petals, ch 3) around, join with sl st in joining sl st on last rnd (8 ch-3 sps).

Rnd 4: Sl st in next ch-3 sp, (ch 2, hdc, dc, hdc, ch 2, sl st) in same sp, (sl st, ch 2, hdc, dc, hdc, ch 2, sl st) in each ch sp around, join with sl st in first sl st.

Rnd 5: Ch 1, sc in first st, ch 4; working behind petals, (sc in second sl st between petals, ch 4) around, join with sl st in first sc, fasten off (8 ch-4 sps).

NOTE: For **beginning cluster (beg cl),** ch 3, *yo 2 times, insert hook in same ch sp, yo, draw lp through, (yo, draw through 2 lps on hook) 2 times; repeat from *, yo, draw through all 3 lps on hook.

For **cluster (cl),** *yo 2 times, insert hook in next ch sp, yo, draw lp through, (yo, draw through 2 lps on hook) 2 times; repeat from * 2 more times in same ch sp, yo, draw through all 4 lps on hook.

Rnd 6: Join med. green with sl st in first ch sp, beg cl, ch 2, cl in same ch sp, ch 2, *(cl, ch 2, cl) in next ch sp, ch 2; repeat from * around, join with sl st in top of beg cl, fasten off (16 ch-2 sps).

Rnd 7: Join dk. green with sc in any ch sp, 2 sc in same sp, 3 sc in each of next 2 ch sps, (hdc, dc, ch 2, dc, hdc) in next ch sp, *3 sc in each of next 3 ch sps, (hdc, dc, ch 2, dc, hdc) in next ch sp; repeat from * around, join with sl st in first sc (52 sts, 4 ch-2 sps).

Rnd 8: Sl st in next st, ch 1, sc in same st, ch 3, skip next st, (sc in next st, ch 3, skip next st) 4 times, (sc, ch 3, sc) in next ch sp, *ch 3, skip next st, (sc in next st, ch 3, skip next st) 6 times, (sc, ch 3, sc) in next ch sp; repeat from * 2 more times, ch 3, skip next st, sc in next st, ch 3, skip last st, join, fasten off (32 ch-3 sps).

Rnd 9: Working behind ch-3 sps of last rnd, in skipped sts and corner ch sps on rnd before last, join med. blue with sl st in first dc after any corner ch sp on rnd 7, ch 3, sl st in **back lp** of center ch on ch-3 sp of rnd 8 directly above skipped dc, dc in same dc on rnd 7, (dc in next skipped st on rnd 7, sl st in **back lp** of center ch of next ch-3 sp on rnd 8, dc in same st as last dc made) 6 times; *[working between sc sts on rnd 8, 2 dc in next ch sp on rnd 7, sl st in **back lp** of center ch on corner ch-3 sp of rnd 8, 2 dc in same ch sp on rnd 7]; repeat between ( ) 7 times; repeat from * 2 more times; repeat between [ ], join with sl st in top of ch-3 (72 dc).

Rnd 10: Ch 1; skipping all sl sts, sc in each dc around with ch-2 above each corner sl st, join with sl st in first sc, fasten off (72 sc, 4 ch-2 sps).

Rnd 11: Join lt. blue with sl st in any corner ch sp, ch 3, (dc, ch 3, 2 dc) in same sp, *[skip next 2 sts, (2 sc in next st, skip next st) 8 times], (2 dc, ch 3, 2 dc) in next corner ch sp; repeat from * 2 more times; repeat between [ ], join with sl st in top of ch-3 (64 sc, 16 dc, 4 ch-3 sps).

Rnd 12: Ch 1, 2 sc in first st, skip next st, *[(2 sc, ch 2, 2 sc) in next ch sp, skip next 2 sts, (2 sc in next st, skip next st) across] to next corner ch sp; repeat from * 2 more times; repeat between [ ], join with sl st in first sc (88 sc, 4 ch-2 sps).

Rnd 13: Ch 1, sc in each st around with (sc, ch 2, sc) in each corner ch sp, join, fasten off (96 sc, 4 ch-2 sps).

Continued on page 154

Blooms

Designer: Sandra Smith

Size: 54" x 63".

Materials: Worsted-weight yarn

purple, green, gold, maroon, lavender, pink, red and berry; G crochet hook or size needed to obtain gauge.

Gauge: Rnds 1-2 of Motif = 2½" across. Each Motif is 4½" across.

Skill Level: ★★ Average

INSTRUCTIONS

FLOWER (make 14 in each color except off-white)

Rnd 1: Ch 5, sl st in first ch to form ring, ch 1, 12 sc in ring, join with sl st in first sc (12 sc).

Rnd 2: Working this rnd in **back lps** only, ch 9, (sl st in next st, ch 9) around, join with sl st in joining sl st of last rnd, fasten off (12 ch lps).

FIRST MOTIF

Rnd 1: With off-white, ch 5, sl st in first ch to form ring, ch 1, 12 sc in ring, join with sl st in first sc (12 sc).

Rnd 2: Working this rnd in **back lps** only, ch 6, (yo, insert hook in same st, yo, draw lp through, yo, draw through 2 lps on hook, skip next st, yo, insert hook in next st, yo, draw lp through, yo, draw through 2 lps on hook, yo, draw through all 3 lps on hook, ch 3) 5 times, yo, insert hook in same st, yo, draw lp through, yo, draw through 2 lps on hook, insert hook in 3rd ch of ch-6, yo, draw through ch and both lps on hook (6 points, 6 ch sps).

Rnd 3: Ch 2, 7 hdc in next ch sp, (hdc in next point, 7 hdc in next ch sp) around, join with sl st in top of ch-2, **turn** (48 hdc).

NOTE: For **picot,** ch 2, sl st in 2nd ch from hook.

Rnd 4: Working this rnd in **front lps** only, ch 1, sc in each of first 3 sts; holding wrong side of first Flower (see Assembly Diagram on page 155 for color) against side of Motif facing you, working through both thicknesses, sc in next st on Motif and in 5th ch of any ch lp on Flower, (sc in each of next 3 sts on Motif; working through both thicknesses, sc in next st on Motif and in 5th ch of next ch lp on Flower) 2 times, *picot; repeat between ( ) 3 times; repeat from * 2 more times, picot, join with sl st in first sc, fasten off.

ASSEMBLY

NOTES: Using the following instructions for One-Side Joined Motif and Two-Side Joined Motif, work and join Motifs according to Assembly Diagram.

For **joining picot,** ch 1, sl st in corresponding picot on designated Motif, ch 1, sl st in first ch on this picot.

ONE-SIDE JOINED MOTIF

Rnds 1-3: Work same rnds of First Motif.

Rnd 4: Using Flower color indicated on diagram, work same as rnd 4 of First Motif around to last picot; to join this Motif to last Motif made, work joining picot, join with sl st in first sc, fasten off.

TWO-SIDE JOINED MOTIF

Rnds 1-3: Repeat same rnds of First Motif.

Rnd 4: Working this rnd in **front lps** only, ch 1, sc in each of first 3 sts; holding wrong side of next Flower against side of Motif facing you, working through both thicknesses, sc in next st on Motif and in 5th ch of any ch lp on Flower, (sc in each of next 3 sts on Motif; working through both thicknesses, sc in next st on Motif and in 5th ch of next ch lp on Flower) 2 times, *picot; repeat between ( ) 3 times; repeat from * one more time; joining to side of last Motif made, work joining picot; repeat between ( ) 3 more times; joining to bottom of corresponding Motif on last row, work joining picot, join with sl st in first sc, fasten off.

FILLER MOTIF

Rnd 1: With off-white, ch 6, sl st in first ch to form ring, ch 1, 16 sc in ring, join with sl st in first sc (16 sc).

Rnd 2: With wrong side of Afghan facing you, working in **back lps** only on Filler Motif, between

Continued on page 155

Berry Garland

Designer: Maggie Weldon

for Monsanto's Designs for America Program

Size: 45" x 66" not including Fringe.

Materials: Worsted weight yarn — 27 oz. grey, 9 oz. each med. blue and dk. rose; I crochet hook or size needed to obtain gauge.

Gauge: 3 dc = 1"; rows 1-3 = 2".

Skill Level: ★★ Average

INSTRUCTIONS

AFGHAN

Row 1: With grey, ch 199, dc in 4th ch from hook, dc in each ch across, turn (197 dc).

Row 2: Ch 4, skip next st, dc in next st, (ch 1, skip next st, dc in next st) across, turn (99 dc, 98 ch sps).

NOTE: For **cross stitch (cr st),** skip next ch sp, dc in next st; working over dc just made, dc in skipped ch sp.

Row 3: Ch 3, cr st across to last ch sp, skip last ch sp, dc in last st, **do not** turn, fasten off.

NOTE: For **popcorn (pc),** 3 dc in same st, drop lp from hook, insert hook in first st of 3-dc group, pick up dropped lp, draw through st. Push to right side of work

Row 4: Join med. blue with sc in first st, *ch 3, (dc, pc, dc) in side of last sc made, skip next 3 sts, sc in next st; repeat from * across, **do not** turn, fasten off.

Row 5: Join grey with sl st in first sc, ch 4, (*sc in 3rd ch of next ch-3, ch 1, skip next pc group, dc in next sc*, ch 1) across to last pc; repeat between **, turn.

Row 6: Ch 4, dc in next sc; skipping ch sps, (ch 1, dc) in each st across, turn.

Row 7: Repeat row 3.

Row 8: With dk. rose, repeat row 4.

Row 9: Join grey with sl st in first sc, ch 4, (*sc in 3rd ch of next ch-3, ch 1, skip next pc group, dc in next sc*, ch 1) across to last pc; repeat between **, turn.

Row 10: Ch 4, dc in next sc; skipping ch sps, (ch 1, dc) in each st across, turn.

Row 11: Repeat row 3.

Rows 12-79: Repeat rows 4-11 consecutively, ending with row 7.

FRINGE

For **each Fringe,** cut 6 strands, each 18" long of color to match row. With all six strands held together, fold in half, insert hook through end of row, draw fold through, draw loose ends through fold, tighten. Trim ends.

Work one Fringe in end of each row across each end of Afghan.✣

Autumn Bounty

continued from page 138

19 sts, skip next st], (3 dc, ch 2, 3 dc) in next corner ch sp; repeat between [ ], join, (108 dc and 9 cls across each short end, 140 dc and 13 cls across each long edge).

Rnd 3: Ch 1, sc in each dc and in each cl around with 3 sc in each corner ch-2 sp, join with sl st in first sc (119 sc across each short end between corner sc, 155 sc across each long edge between corner sc).

Rnds 4-8: Ch 1, sc in each st around with 3 sc in center st of each 3-sc corner, join with sl st in first sc, ending with 129 sc across each short end between corner sc and 165 sc across each long edge between corner sc. At end of last rnd, fasten off.

Rnd 9: Join CC with sc in any center corner st, 4 sc in same st, *skip next 3 sts, (3 sc in next st, skip next 2 sts) across to next center corner st, 5 sc in next corner st; repeat from * 2 more times, skip next 3 sts, (3 sc in next st, skip next 2 sts) across, join with sl st in first sc, fasten off.✣

Pepper Patch

continued from page 141

ing picot, skip next 2 sts on this Motif, (sc in next st, joining picot, skip next 2 sts on this Motif) across to next center corner st, hdc in next st; joining to next corner picot, work joining picot, hdc in same st on last rnd of this Motif, picot, *skip next 2 sts, (sc in next st, picot, skip next 2 sts) across to next center corner st, (hdc, picot, hdc) in next st, picot; repeat from * 2 more times, join with sl st in 2nd ch of ch-4, fasten off (37 picots, 13 joined petals).

Repeat Second Motif 4 more times for a total of 6 Motifs.

SECOND ROW

First Motif

Rnds 1-11: Repeat same rnds of First Row's First Motif.

Rnd 12: Joining to side of First Motif as shown in diagram, repeat same rnd of First Row's Second Motif.

Second Motif

Rnds 1-11: Repeat same rnds of First Row's First Motif.

Rnd 12: Join green with sl st in center st of first 3-sc group; joining to side of next Motif on last Row made, work beg joining picot, hdc in same st on this Motif, *joining picot, skip next 2 sts, (sc in next st, joining picot, skip next 2 sts) across to next center corner st, hdc in next st, joining picot, hdc in same st on this Motif*; joining to bottom of last Motif made on this Row; repeat between **, [joining picot, skip next 2 sts, (sc in next st, picot, skip next 2 sts) across to next center corner st], (hdc, picot, hdc) in next st; repeat between [ ], join with sl st in 2nd ch of ch-4, fasten off (26 joined picots, 24 picots).

Repeat Second Motif 4 more times for a total of 6 Motifs.

Repeat Second Row 3 more times for a total of 5 Rows.

EDGING

Working around entire outer edge, join burnt orange with sc in 2nd ch of ch-4 on any corner picot, ◊[picot, sc in 4th ch of ch-4 on same picot, picot, *(sc in 3rd ch of ch-4 on next picot, picot) across to next joined picots, hdc in side of sc on next joined picot, picot; repeat from * across to last Motif on this side, (sc in 3rd ch of ch-4 on next petal, picot) across] to next corner petal, sc in 2nd ch of ch-4 on next corner petal; repeat from ◊ 2 more times; repeat between [ ], join with sl st in first sc, fasten off.✣

JOINING DIAGRAM

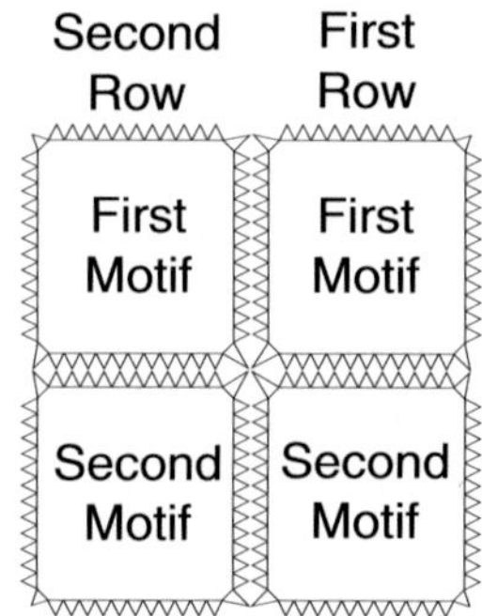

Stawberry Fantasies —

continued from page 144

(skip next 2 sts, shell in next st, skip next 2 sts, sc in next st) 4 times; repeat from * 2 more times; repeat between [ ], (shell in next st, skip next 2 sts, sc in next st, skip next 2 sts) 2 times, join, fasten off (24 shells, 24 sc).

Rnd 10: Join pink with sc in ch sp of first shell, ch 4, cl in next sc, ch 4, (sc in ch sp of next shell, ch 4, cl in next sc, ch 4) 2 times, *[(cl, ch 5, cl) in ch sp of next corner shell, ch 4, cl in next sc, ch 4], (sc in ch sp of next shell, ch 4, cl in next sc, ch 4) 5 times; repeat from * 2 more times; repeat between [ ], (sc in ch sp of next shell, ch 4, cl in next sc, ch 4) 2 times, join with sl st in first sc, fasten off (48 ch-4 sps, 4 ch-5 sps).

Rnd 11: Join white with sc in first ch-4 sp, ch 4, (sc in next ch-4 sp, ch 4) 5 times, (sc, ch 7, sc) in next corner ch-5 sp, ch 4, *(sc in next ch-4 sp, ch 4) 12 times, (sc, ch 7, sc) in next corner ch-5 sp, ch 4; repeat from * 2 more times, (sc in next ch-4 sp, ch 4) 6 times, join, fasten off (52 ch-4 sps, 4 ch-7 lps).

Second Block

Rnds 1-10: Repeat same rnds of First Block.

Rnd 11: Join white with sc in first ch-4 sp, ch 4, (sc in next ch-4 sp, ch 4) 5 times, *(sc, ch 7, sc) in next corner ch-5 sp, ch 4, (sc in next ch-4 sp, ch 4) 12 times; repeat from * one more time; to **join,** joining to side of last Block (see Joining Diagram), sc in next corner ch-5 sp, ch 3, sc in corresponding ch-5 sp on last Block, ch 3, sc in same ch-5 sp on this Block, ch 2, sc in next ch-4 sp on last Block, ch 2, (sc in next ch-4 sp on this Block, ch 2, sc in next ch-4 sp on last Block, ch 2) 12 times, sc in next corner ch-5 sp on this Block, ch 3, sc in next corner ch-5 sp on last Block, ch 3, sc in same ch-5 sp on this Block; ch 4, (sc in next ch-4 sp, ch 4) 6 times, join, fasten off.

Repeat Seacond Block one more time for a total of three Blocks.

SECOND ROW

First Block

Joining to bottom of First Block on last row, work same as First Row Second Block.

Second Block

Rnds 1-10: Repeat same rnds of First Row's First Block.

Rnd 11: Join white with sc in first ch-4 sp, ch 4, (sc in next ch-4 sp, ch 4) 5 times, (sc, ch 7, sc) in next corner ch-5 sp, ch 4, (sc in next ch-4 sp, ch 4) 12 times; to **join,** joining to bottom of next Block on last row, *sc in next corner ch-5 sp, ch 3, sc in corresponding ch-5 sp on other Block, ch 3, sc in same ch-5 sp on this Block, ch 2, sc in next ch-4 sp on other Block, ch 2, (sc in next ch-4 sp on this Block, ch 2, sc in next ch-4 sp on other Block, ch 2) 12 times*, joining to side of last Block on this row; repeat between **, sc in next corner ch-5 sp on this Block, ch 3, sc in next corner ch-5 sp on other Block, ch 3, sc in same ch sp on this Block; ch 4, (sc in next ch-4 sp, ch 4) 6 times, join, fasten off.

Repeat Second Block one more time for a total of three Blocks.

Repeat Second Row two more time for a total of four rows.

BORDER

Rnd 1: Working around entire outer edge, join white with sc in any corner ch-7 lp, ch 5, sc in same lp, ch 4, (sc in next ch sp, ch 4) across to next corner ch-7 lp, *(sc, ch 5, sc) in next ch-7 lp, ch 4, (sc in next ch sp, ch 4) across to next corner ch-7 lp; repeat from * around, join with sl st in first sc, fasten off.

Rnd 2: Join pink with sl st in first corner ch-5 sp, (beg cl, ch 4, cl) in same sp, ch 4, (cl, ch 4) in each ch-4 sp around with (cl, ch 4, cl, ch 4) in each corner ch-5 sp, join with sl st in top of beg cl, fasten off.✣

JOINING DIAGRAM

First Row	First Block	Second Block
Second Row	First Block	Second Block

Crimson Carnations —

continued from page 147

ASSEMBLY

Holding 2 Blocks right sides together, working through both thicknesses, join lt. blue with *sc in first corner ch sp, sc in each st across to next corner ch sp, sc in next ch sp*; [holding 2 more Blocks together, ch 1; repeat between **]; repeat between [ ] 5 more times, joining a total of 7 pairs of Blocks, fasten off.

Repeat with remaining Blocks, making 5 joined rows of 7 Blocks each until all Blocks are joined vertically.

Join all Blocks horizontally in same manner.

BORDER

Rnd 1: Working around entire outer edge, join lt. blue with sc in first sc after any corner ch-2 sp, *(sc in each sc across to next ch-2 sp before seam, hdc in next joined ch-2 sp, hdc in seam, hdc in in next joined ch-2 sp) across to last Block on this side, sc in each sc across to next corner ch sp, (sc, ch 2, sc) in next ch sp; repeat from * around, join with sl st in first sc, fasten off (134 sc across each short end, 188 sc across each long edge, 4 corner ch sps).

NOTE: If Afghan begins to ruffle when working next rnd, change to next smaller size crochet hook.

Rnd 2: Join med. green with sc in any corner ch sp, ch 3, sc in same sp, ◊[skip next 2 sts, *(sc, ch 3, sc) in next st, skip next st; repeat from * across to next corner ch sp], (sc, ch 3, sc) in next ch sp; repeat from ◊ 2 more times; repeat between [ ], join, **turn,** fasten off.

NOTE: For **decrease (dec),** yo, insert hook in next st, yo, draw lp through, insert hook in next st, yo, draw lp through, yo, draw through 3 lps on hook, yo, draw through last 2 lps on hook.

Rnd 3: Join dk. green with sl st in any corner ch sp, ch 3, (dc, ch 2, 2 dc) in same sp, *[dec, (sc in next ch sp, dec) across to next corner ch sp], (2 dc, ch 2, 2 dc) in next ch sp; repeat from * 2 more times; repeat between [ ], join with sl st in top of ch-3, **do not** turn, fasten off.

Rnd 4: Join med. blue with sc in any corner ch sp, (3 dc, sc) in same sp, ◊[skip next dc, (sc, dc, sc) in next dc, (sc, dc, sc) in next dec, *skip next sc, (sc, dc, sc) in next dec; repeat from * across to last 2 dc before next corner ch sp, (sc, dc, sc) in next dc, skip next dc], (sc, 3 dc, sc) in next corner ch sp; repeat from ◊ 2 more times; repeat between [ ], join with sl st in first sc, fasten off.✣

Lattice Blooms

continued from page 148

LATTICE BLOOMS FILLER MOTIF DIAGRAM

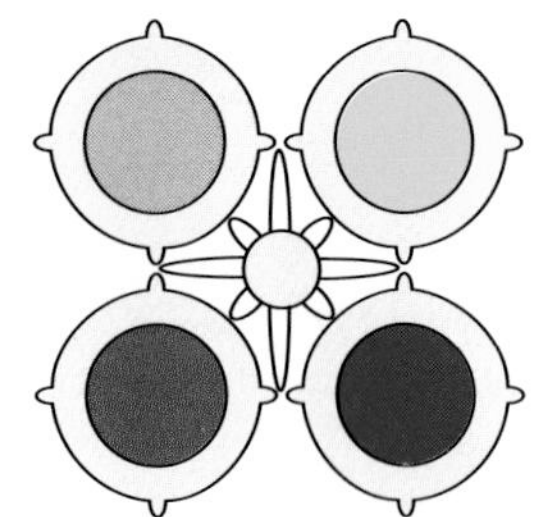

four joined Motifs (see Filler Motif Diagram), *[ch 2, sl st in 6th sc between joining picots, ch 1, sl st in 2nd ch of ch-2, ch 1, skip next st on Filler Motif, sl st in next st, ch 4, sl st in next joining sl st between Motifs, ch 1, sl st in 4th ch of ch-4, ch 3, skip next st on Filler Motif], sl st in next st; repeat from * 2 more times; repeat between [ ], join with sl st in joining sl st on last rnd, fasten off.

Repeat Filler Motif in spaces between all joined Motifs.✣

LATTICE BLOOMS ASSEMBLY DIAGRAM

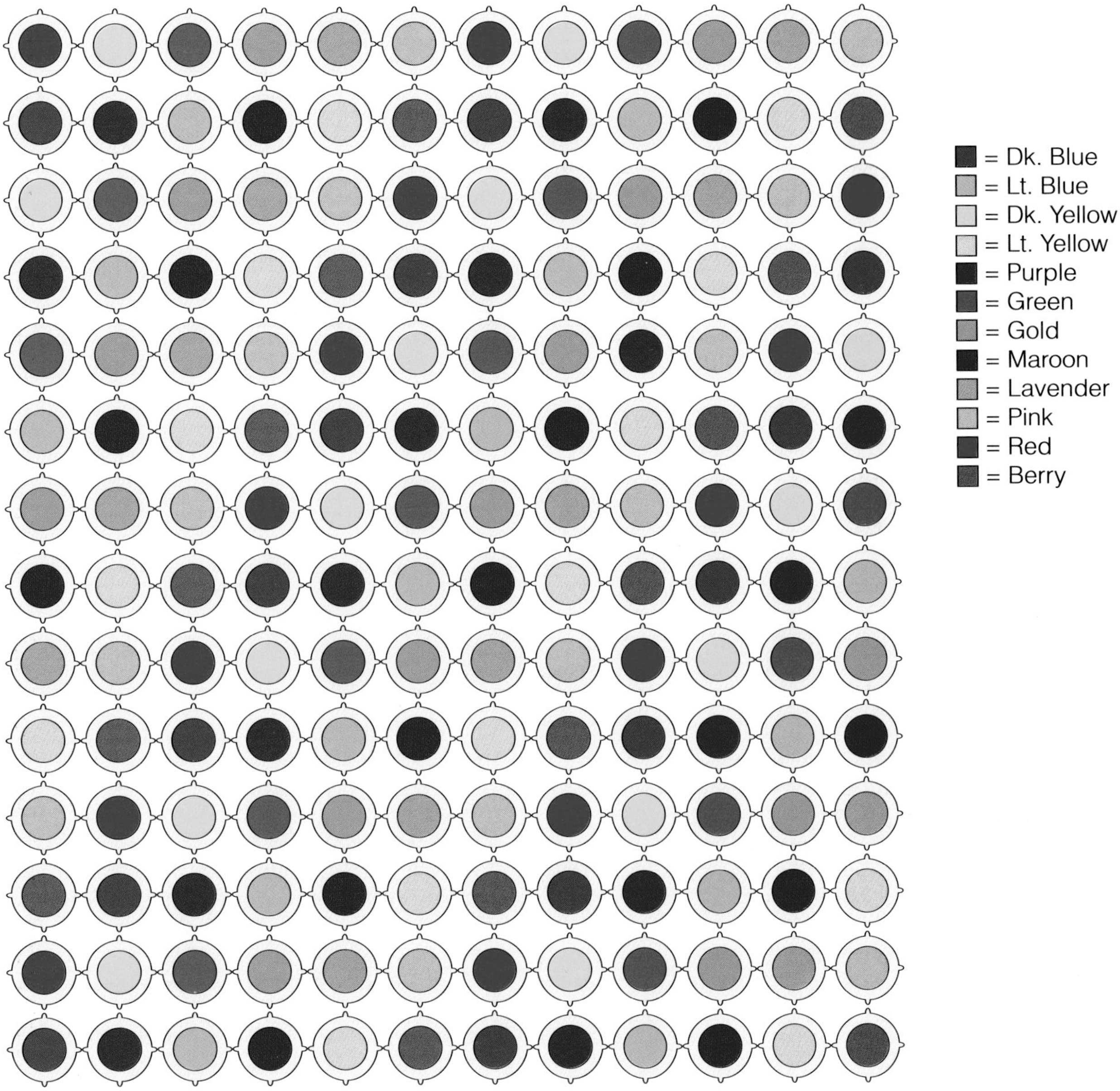

= Dk. Blue
= Lt. Blue
= Dk. Yellow
= Lt. Yellow
= Purple
= Green
= Gold

= Maroon
= Lavender
= Pink
= Red
= Berry

Getting Started

Yarn & Hooks

Always use the weight of yarn specified in the pattern so you can be assured of achieving the proper gauge. It is best to purchase at least one extra skein of each color needed to allow for differences in tension and dyes.

The hook size stated in the pattern is to be used as a guide. Always work a swatch of an afghan's stitch pattern with the suggested hook size. If you find your gauge is smaller or larger than what is specified, choose a different size hook.

Gauge

Gauge is measured by counting the number of rows or stitches per inch. Each of the afghans featured in this book will have a gauge listed. Gauge for some small motifs or flowers is given as an overall measurement. Proper gauge must be attained for the afghan to come out the size stated, and to prevent ruffling and puckering.

Make a swatch about 4" square in the stitch indicated in the gauge section of the instructions. Lay the swatch flat and measure the stitches. If you have more stitches per inch than specified in the pattern, your gauge is too tight and you need a larger hook. Fewer stitches per inch indicates a gauge that is too loose. In this case, choose a smaller hook size. Next, check the number of rows. If necessary, adjust your row gauge slightly by pulling the loops down a little tighter on your hook, or by pulling the loops up slightly to extend them.

Once you've attained the proper gauge, you're ready to start your afghan. Remember to check your gauge periodically to avoid problems later.

Pattern Repeat Symbols

Written crochet instructions typically include symbols such as parentheses, asterisks and brackets. In some patterns a diamond or bullet (dot), may be added.

( ) Parentheses enclose instructions which are to be worked again later or the number of times indicated after the parentheses. For example, "(2 dc in next st, skip next st) 5 times" means to follow the instructions within the parentheses a total of five times. If no number appears after the parentheses, you will be instructed when to repeat further into the pattern. Parentheses may also be used to enclose a group of stitches which should be worked in one space or stitch. For example, "(2 dc, ch 2, 2 dc) in next st" means to work all the stitches within the parentheses in the next stitch.

* Asterisks may be used alone or in pairs, usually in combination with parentheses. If used in pairs, the instructions enclosed within asterisks will be followed by instructions for repeating. These repeat instructions may appear later in the pattern or immediately after the last asterisk. For example, "*Dc in next 4 sts, (2 dc, ch 2, 2 dc) in corner sp*, dc in next 4 sts; repeat between ** 2 more times" means to work through the instructions up to the word "repeat," then repeat only the instructions that are enclosed within the asterisks twice.

If used alone an asterisk marks the beginning of instructions which are to be repeated. Work through the instructions from the beginning, then repeat only the portion after the * up to the word "repeat"; then follow any remaining instructions. If a number of times is given, work through the instructions one time, repeat the number of times stated, then follow the remainder of the instructions.

[ ] Brackets, ◊ diamonds and • bullets are used in the same manner as asterisks. Follow the specific instructions given when repeating.

Finishing

Patterns that require assembly will suggest a tapestry needle in the materials. This should be a #16 or #18 blunt-tipped tapestry needle. When stitching pieces together, be careful to keep the seams flat so pieces do not pucker.

Hiding loose ends is never a fun task, but if done correctly, will keep your afghan looking great for years. Always leave 6-8" of yarn when beginning or ending. Thread the loose end into your tapestry needle and carefully weave through the back of several stitches. Then, weave in the opposite direction, going through different strands. Gently pull the end and clip, allowing the end to pull up under the stitches.

If your afghan needs blocking, a light steam pressing works well. Lay your afghan on a large table or on the floor, shaping and smoothing by hand as much as possible. Adjust your steam iron to the permanent press setting, then hold slightly above the stitches, allowing the steam to penetrate the yarn. Do not rest the iron on the afghan. Allow to dry completely.

SKILL LEVEL REQUIREMENTS:

Easy — Requires knowledge of basic skills only; great for beginners or anyone who wants quick results.

Average — Requires some experience; very comfortable for accomplished stitchers, yet suitable for beginners wishing to expand their abilities.

Advanced — Requires a high level of skill in all areas; average stitchers may find some areas of these patterns difficult, though still workable.

Challenging — Requires advance skills in both technique and comprehension, as well as a daring spirit; some areas may present difficulty for even the most accomplished stitchers.

For More Information

Sometimes even the most experienced needlecrafters can find themselves having trouble following instructions. If you have difficulty completing your project, write to:

Afghan Inspirations Editors
The Needlecraft Shop
23 Old Pecan Road, Big Sandy, Texas 75755

Acknowledgments

Our sincerest thanks and appreciation goes to the following manufacturers for generously providing their product for use in the following projects:

COATS & CLARK

Heather Mist	Brunswick Windmist
Lacy Trellis	Red Heart Super Saver
Spring Compote	Red Heart Jeweltones
Morning Glory	Red Heart Super Saver
Dresden Plate	Brunswick Windrush
Creme de Menthe	Brunswick Windrush
Royal Satin	Paton's Canadiana
Queen's Lace	J. & P. Coats Acrylic Thread
Regal Tapestry	Red Heart Super Saver

LION BRAND

Roses At Midnight	Jiffy
Imperial Jade	Jiffy
Heavenly Luster	Wool Ease
Peacock Petals	Jiffy

CARON INTERNATIONAL

Afternoon Tea	Simply Soft
Evening Glow	Simply Soft
After The Rain	Wintuk
Crystal Pleasure	Simply Soft
Wisteria Wonder	Wintuk
Nature's Palette	Wintuk
Spring Meadows	Simply Soft
Crimson Carnations	Simply Soft

SPINRITE

Rippling Brook	Bernat Berella "4"
Jeweled Sky	Bernat Berella "4"
Cascading Light	Bernat Nice n Soft
Dainty Delight	Bernat Berella "4"
Northern Lights	Bernat Berella "4"
Midnight Glow	Bernat Berella "4"
Lavender Bouquet	Bernat Berella "4"
Antique Poppies	Bernat Berella "4"
Summer Sage	Bernat Berella "4"
Berry Garden	Bernat Berella "4"

East Texas Photography Locations & Credits

Cover photograph: at the home of Rochelle Boyce, Gladewater.
Other locations: Big Sandy – *Ambassador College*, Marvin & Naomi Harmdierks; Hawkins – Dale Miller; Kilgore – Lloyd & Evelyn Bolding, *Danville Farms*, Craig & Jan Jaynes, Corine Camp Odom; Mt. Pleasant – Dana & Marianne Havron, *Tankersley Gardens*; Tyler – Ed & Elaine Snavely.
Other photographs: Mary Van de Ven, Hawaii; and Image ©1997 PhotoDisc, Inc.
Props: *The Beary Patch*, Patricia Pickle, Kilgore; *Georgia's Plants*, White Oak; Rudy Beloney, Big Sandy.
Models: Jessica Chaffin, Courtney Hitt, Bonne and Savanna Reed.

Stitch Guide

BASIC STITCHES

1 Front Loop (A)/Back Loop (B)
(front lp/back lp)

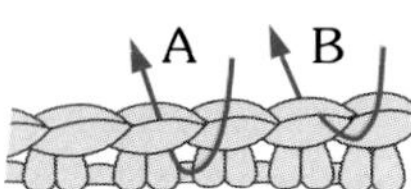

2 Chain
(ch)

Yo, draw hook through lp.

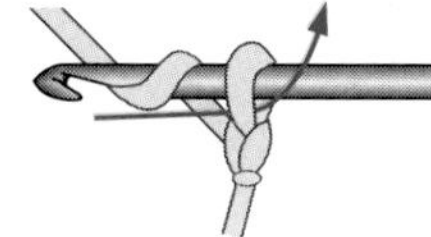

3 Slip Stitch
(sl st)

Insert hook in st, yo, draw through st and lp on hook.

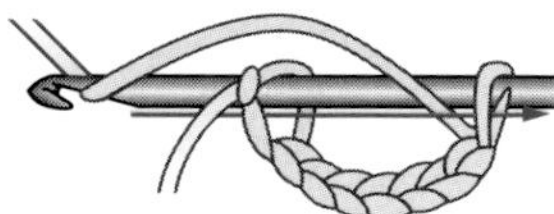

4 Single Crochet
(sc)

Insert hook in st (A), yo, draw lp through, yo, draw through both lps on hook (B).

A

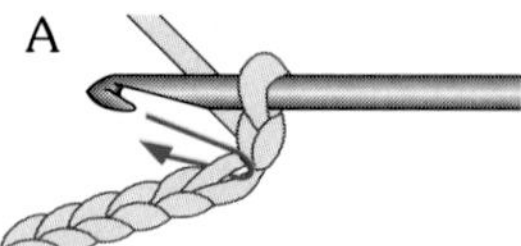

B

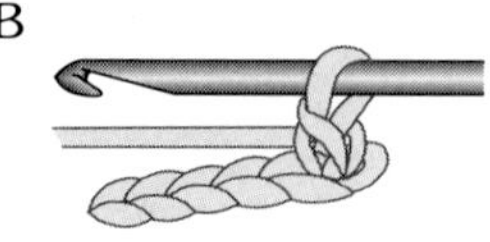

5 Half Double Crochet
(hdc)

Yo, insert hook in st (A), yo, draw lp through (B), yo, draw through all 3 lps on hook (C).

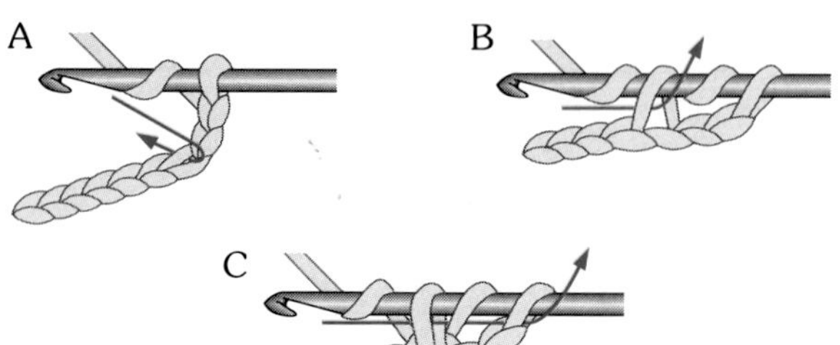

6 Double Crochet
(dc)

Yo, insert hook in st (A), yo, draw lp through (B), (yo, draw through 2 lps on hook) 2 times (C and D).

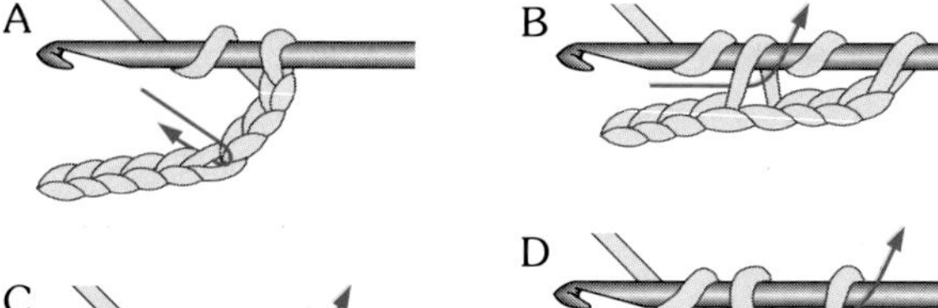

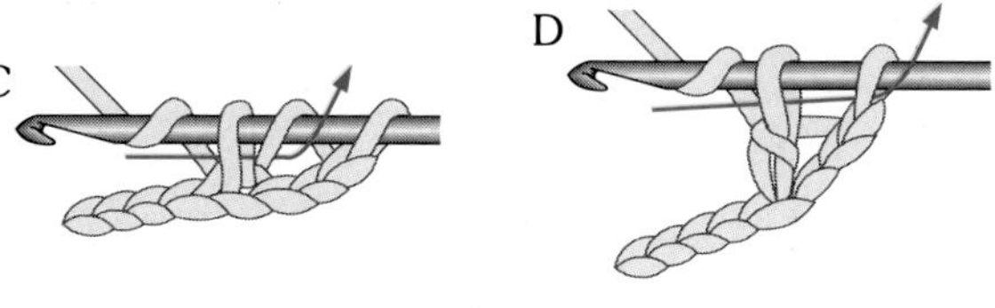

7 Treble Crochet
(tr)

Yo 2 times, insert hook in st (A), yo, draw lp through (B), (yo, draw through 2 lps on hook) 3 times (C, D and E).

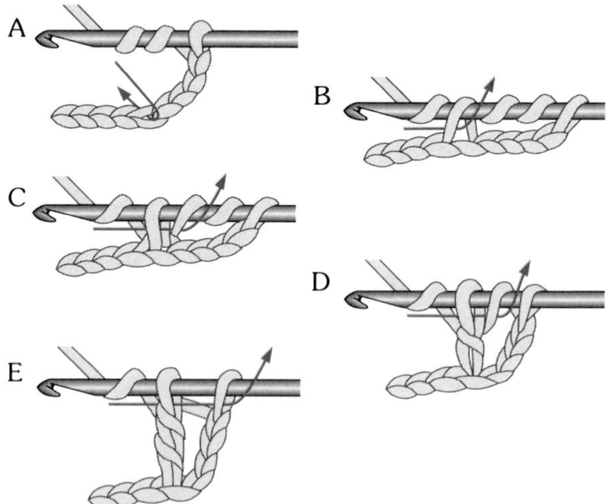

Standard Stitch Abbreviations

ch(s)	chain(s)
dc	double crochet
dtr	double treble crochet
hdc	half double crochet
lp(s)	loop(s)
rnd(s)	round(s)
sc	single crochet
sl st	slip stitch
sp(s)	space(s)
st(s)	stitch(es)
tog	together
tr	treble crochet
tr tr	triple treble crochet
yo	yarn over

8 Double Treble Crochet *(dtr)*

Yo 3 times, insert hook in st (A), yo, draw lp through (B), (yo, draw through 2 lps on hook) 4 times (C, D, E and F).

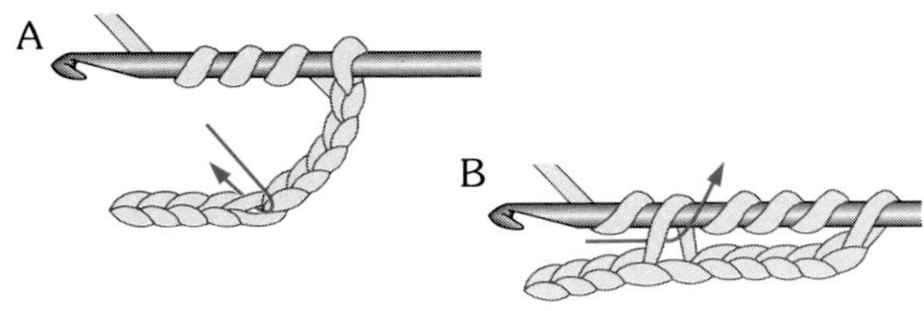

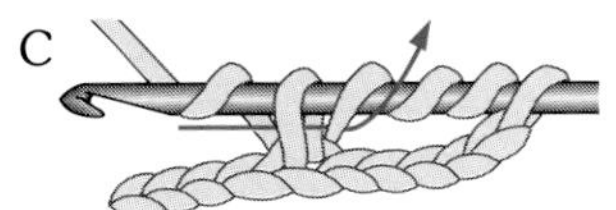

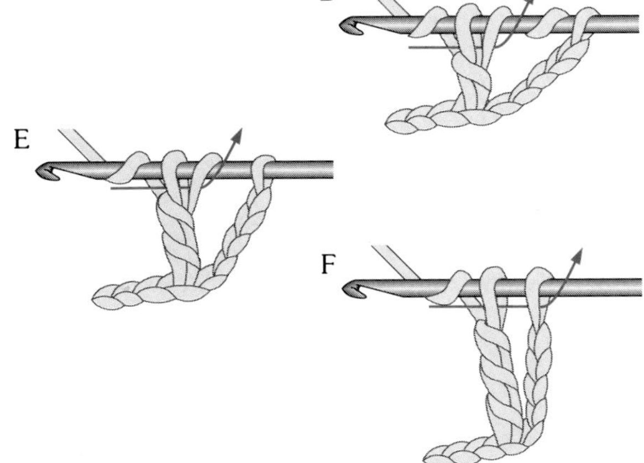

SPECIAL STITCHES

Front Post/Back Post Stitches *(fp/bp)*

Yo, insert hook from front to back (A) or back to front (B) around post of st on indicated row; complete as stated in pattern.

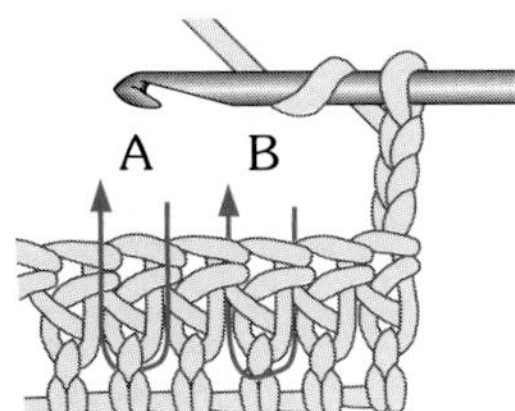

Reverse Single Crochet *(reverse sc)*

Working from left to right, insert hook in next st to the right (A), yo, draw through st, complete as sc (B).

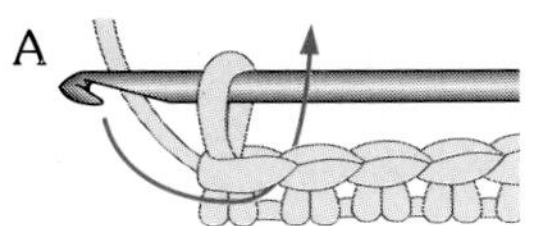

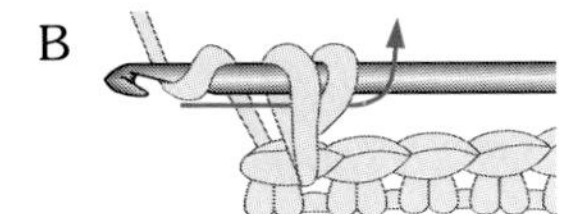

CHANGING COLORS

Single Crochet Color Change *(sc color change)*

Drop first color; yo with 2nd color, draw through last 2 lps of st.

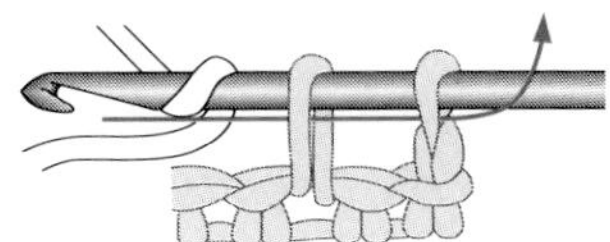

Double Crochet Color Change *(dc color change)*

Drop first color; yo with 2nd color, draw through last 2 lps of st.

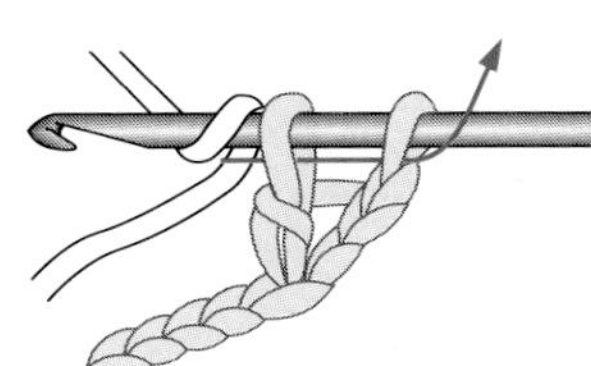

DECREASING

Single Crochet next 2 stitches together *(sc next 2 sts tog)*

Draw up lp in each of next 2 sts, yo, draw through all 3 lps on hook.

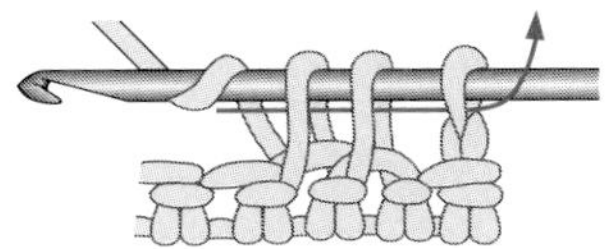

Half Double Crochet next 2 stitches together *(hdc next 2 sts tog)*

(Yo, insert hook in next st, yo, draw lp through) 2 times, yo, draw through all 5 lps on hook.

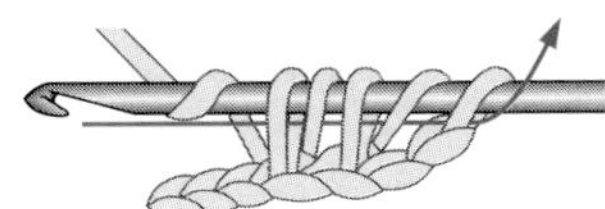

Double Crochet next 2 stitches together *(dc next 2 sts tog)*

(Yo, insert hook in next st, yo, draw lp through, yo, draw through 2 lps on hook) 2 times, yo, draw through all 3 lps on hook.

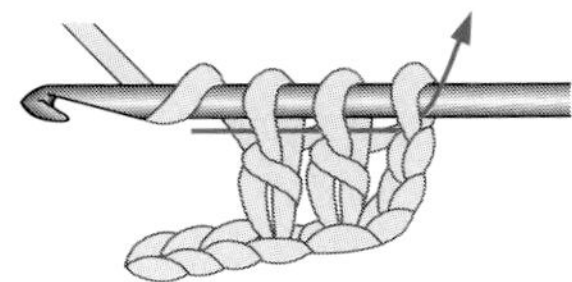

Index

Designers